SYMBOL AND REALITY

B3216
C34
H3

CARL H. HAMBURG

SYMBOL AND REALITY

Studies in the philosophy of

Ernst Cassirer

MARTINUS NIJHOFF / THE HAGUE / 1956

66240

Copyright 1956 by Martinus Nijhoff, The Hague, Netherlands
All rights reserved, including the right to translate or to
reproduce this book or parts thereof in any form

PRINTED IN THE NETHERLANDS

THIS BOOK IS DEDICATED TO
MY MOTHER AND LONA

PREFACE

Since prefaces, for the most part, are written after a book is done, yet face the reader before he gets to it, it is perhaps not surprising that we usually find ourselves addressed by a more chastened and qualifying author than we eventually encounter in the ensuing pages. It is, after all, not only some readers, but the writer of a book himself who reads what he has done and failed to do. If the above is the rule, I am no exception to it.

The discerning reader need not be told that the following studies differ, not only in the approaches they make to their unifying subject-matter, but also in their precision and thus adequacy of presentation. In addition to the usual reasons for this rather common shortcoming, there is an another one in the case of the present book. In spite of its comparative brevity, the time-span between its inception and termination covers some twenty years. As a result, some (historical and epistemological) sections reflect my preoccupation with CASSI-RER's early works during student days in Germany and France. When, some ten years later, CASSIRER in a letter expressed "great joy" and anticipation for a more closely supervised continuation of my efforts (which, because of his untimely death, never came to pass), he gave me all the encouragement needed to go to work on a critical exposition of his "symbolic form" concept.

Since then, the book was re-written, partly pruned and partly expanded. This process, I am sure, could have gone on without damage to the manuscript, for years to come. Instead, overcoming the double vanities of publishing one's thoughts either too fast or not at all, the book is now readied in the hope that, even as it stands, it may serve as a somewhat more sustained examination of the philosophy of CASSIRER than is available so far.

Edward G. Ballard, Richard L. Barber, Irwin Edman, James Gutman, Suzanne K. Langer, Eric Lenneberg, Ernest Nagel and

John E. Smith, by criticism or suggestion, have helped to improve such parts of this book as they have read.

Thanks are due to *The Library of Living Philosophers* (Northwestern University), *The Journal of Philosophy* and *The Tulane Studies in Philosophy* for permission to use some material previously published in their pages. Due acknowledgments to publishers from whose publications I have quoted will be itemized in the bibliography.

CARL H. HAMBURG

TABLE OF CONTENTS

INTRODUCTION

1

As one moves into the second half of the twentieth century, backward glances over failures and achievements of the first half are hard to suppress. Depending upon what one is considering, different appraisals will be in order, ranging all the way from exultation to disillusionment or total indifference. What is the situation in regard to "the philosophy of our time"? Or better: what can one significantly say about it in all brevity?

(1) On one conclusion both professional and non-professional observers may agree: while there are a good many philosophers about, there is at this time hardly yet anything sufficiently unified about their thinking to warrant the belief in the existence of a "contemporary philosophy" as a meaningful unit of classification. This is to make more than the trivial assertion that in the years since the turn of the century philosophers have failed any more markedly than at other periods to come out with one single rather than a variety of more or less systematically connected conclusions on this presumably self-same world. The difficulty is rather with finding a set of characteristics which could serve as a criterion for deciding for any given philosophy whether it is – in approach, method, outlook or concern – of the "contemporary" kind or not. Supposing one were to construct such a criterion by concentrating on what one takes to be peculiar to our rather than to any previous age. Reference could then be made to the therapeutical purpose of the logical positivist, the social control outlook of the pragmatist, the destiny-preoccupation of the existentialist. To define "20th Century"-philosophy in terms consonant with these three currents of thought would merely require specification of their common denominator. But even supposing that such a denominator could be found and formulated as a common secular, practical and individualistic concern, what would one have achieved? We would have a

definition too narrow to account for some of the most effective
and widely-held philosophies of our time which, such as Dialectical Materialism and Neo-Thomism, are either not individualistic or not secular in orientation. In order to broaden our classification, we could, of course, push on to even more ultimate
concerns such as, e.g., the contemporary philosopher's preoccupation with science, its method, reach and limitation; or his
"quest for certainty" in a world rendered insecure by divided
loyalties; or, finally, his self-consciousness in point of method
and "justification". But we now would have avoided the danger
of being narrow-minded only at the expense of creating a class so
large that it would generously accommodate all that has ever
historically appeared as an instance of the sort of reflection known
as philosophy. A choice has thus to be made. Either one will
dignify with the title "contemporary philosophy" only those
intellectual efforts which are actuated by thought-motives
peculiar to our, the 20th, rather than to any other century; or
one will have to be satisfied with a purely chronological connotation of the term, making reference to all those philosophers,
whether modern in outlook or not, whose work has been and is
being done in this century.

(2) What is said above permits of formulation in a highly
paradoxical form: to the extent that 20th century philosophy
proceeds in a manner markedly different from that of previous
philosophical schools, it has (pragmatism excepted) had little,
if any, effect upon its non-professional contemporaries; while
to the extent that it has commanded the attention of its more or
less enlightened contemporaries, it has (as Dialectical Materialism, Neo-Thomism and Oriental philosophies) remained intellectually dependant upon thought-systems characteristic of earlier
ages. Between the two extremes, there barely manages to survive
a small group of metaphysicians who share the fate of the popu-
lar philosophical movements in not being taken very seriously
by their professional colleagues (because of the metaphorical and
un-scientific vagueness of their pronouncements) while, at the
same time, sharing the fate of the up-to-date sign-analysts in
being ignored by non-professional contemporaries (because of
their aloofness from the pressing problems of the day.) There
opens up the fatal alternative for the 20th century philosopher

of either remaining incomprehensible to his non-professional contemporaries or to be marked as trivial by his professional colleagues. Is there an alternative to this sad predicament?

(3) It may be best to start off with an acknowledgment of the various claims made upon the philosopher. As a specialist in matters of the most general, he has been and must continue to be an inquirer into the grounds and presuppositions of shared beliefs. Analysis as clarification of meaning, rather than discovery or expression of new facts or values, remains an important part of his characteristic contribution to those who aim at an understanding of both what it is that the sciences and the arts discover or express and the method and validation by which their discoveries and expressions may be obtained and confirmed. In consequence, there can be no objection at all to the insistence of the logical positivists during the last few decades upon greater consciousness and control of precise reference by symbols in general and the written or spoken word in particular. The point to be borne in mind, however, is that while it is recommendable for the logician to be thus preoccupied with matters of syntax, semantics and general methodology, as a philosopher he is not yet done. It is still incumbent upon him to use his newly acquired precision tools beyond the realm of artificial or simplified natural and scientific sign-systems. There is also no denying the frequent claim that the philosopher is responsible to his contemporaries for the reasoned discharge of his social responsibilities. To acknowledge this invitation, however, is quite synonymous with asserting that the philosopher must, among other things, also function as a responsible citizen. But what he can do in his capacity as a philosopher for his less articulate and more narrowly specialized fellow-citizens would still seem to be something more than that. Wherever he is successful, he could help them comprehend what is at stake by clarifying for them what is implied by their various and often tangled commitments and beliefs.

He can do so, as a philosopher, not only because, as an analyst of meaning, he can disentangle what only too often turn out to be verbal confusions rather than genuine problems, but also because, not being a scientist, he can, at least, avoid the one-eyed approach of the specialist and, at most, present as circumspect and balanced an analysis of significant intellectual, moral or social issues as is possible on the basis of selected and relevant evidence.

(4) The advice to the 20th century philosopher, coming from his positivist colleagues, namely to labor patiently in the garden of sign-analysis, while justly addressing him as logician, leaves as much of his characteristically philosophical function untouched as the advice, coming from his socially conscious contemporaries, addressed to him as a citizen, namely to leave behind the academic niceties in order to take an active part in whatever is taken to be the burning question of the day. The obvious manner, it would seem, in which, as a philosopher, he can discharge both responsibilities at once would be to exert what logical and linguistic acumen he owns on matters which are not any more nor any less directly related to the problems of his time than is any proper understanding of an issue to its effective resolution.

(5) The point just made is, or should be, commonplace; it is confirmable by however cursory a glance at the history of philosophy. The philosophers who "count" somehow always turn out to be those who, in however indirect a manner, "accounted" for problems which were (culturally, if not physically) significant for beings other than the philosophers themselves. To say that is indeed to enunciate the tautology that unless a philosopher engages in such "accounting", he is to be excluded from the class of philosophers who "count". If one will judge the relative "greatness" of a philosophy by criteria such as "influence" and "fecundity" rather than mere "logical consistency" or "technical rigor", one will, of course, always find that the great philosophers are those who addressed themselves to life-size problems. This is not the same as to say that unless a philosopher finds a responsive age, he could not possibly be a great philosopher. It does make good sense, however, to say that unless a philosopher has been responsive to some of the intellectual or moral or religious issues of his time, unless he could address himself to problems which could touch, move or confuse men, he has, as a rule, no chance whatever to be relevant to men of his or any other age.

(6) The seemingly strange circumstance that only a philosophy which does take seriously problems at a given time has a chance of remaining significant at other times, that the only way to speak through the ages is to have listened and spoken to one's

own age, loses its strangeness if one considers that there are beyond those aspects of the human situation which are peculiar to one group at a time, other aspects which hold for some groups at all times or for all groups at some times, if not indeed, for all groups at all times.

(7) To read a philosophy in context, to evaluate it by considering its relevancy to the historical problem-situation out of which it grew, is, to be sure, not the only legitimate way in which to study its merit. Problems, theoretical or moral, and the manner of dealing with them, may be lifted out of their temporal frame to be evaluated in terms of the varying degrees of technical adequacy involved in their progressive resolution. But if there exists indeed what has been called a cumulative, technical, philosophical knowledge, it is well to remember that just as this knowledge was touched off by the necessity of having to deal with problems larger than technical ones, its mastery is in turn justified only to the extent that it is turned into philosophical work on issues larger than its own technical perfection.

(8) All this is not said to advocate an end to the "honing of the knives" or the "tuning of the musical instruments". There is no merit in being impatient and in ruling out all further "preparatory tasks" in philosophy so that the universe may be "cut at the proper joints" or the speculative symphony finally be played. The tuning and honing, the inquiring into the formal and methodological conditions of sense-making is exactly one of the defining tasks of any, including 20th century, philosophy. To grant this, however, is not to excuse anybody but the specialist from wielding his sharpened tools on issues of human significance. As a philosopher, if not as a logician, his is the opportunity to bring both analytical precision and imaginative synthesis to bear on the whole range of theoretical and moral, social, aesthetic and religious problems, in order to make for more intelligible understanding and intelligent conduct at an age which, at its own peril, cannot yet list its philosophy as one of its more worthwhile achievements.

(9) Contrasted with this demand, 20th century philosophers have not always lived up to their calling. If their voices have been heard beyond the campus, they simply have not sounded true and up to the professional standards of their more cautious

colleagues. The philosophies of Marxism, Catholicism and Existentialism enjoy less hospitality in our departments of philosophy than elsewhere. Our professionally respectable philosophers, on the other hand, remain the great "unknowns" to anybody but their colleagues and students. Some philosophies of previous ages appear to have achieved a somewhat more satisfying balance between relevancy and reliability. This is not to deny the impressive advances which contemporary symbolic logicians have made over any previous "system of logic", nor the liquidation or solution of many a philosophical, genuine or pseudo, problem by a logically more acute and better informed epistemology or methodology. What is to be denied, however, is that any of the language- and science- conscious schools of thought which, as pragmatism, neo-Kantianism and positivism, have distinguished themselves in making such advances possible, constitute, for this reason, a circumspect, balanced and effective philosophy for our time.

(10) It is true that pragmatism had made a hopeful beginning decades ago, and to judge from its occasional programmatic declarations of good intentions, there is promise of more important things to come. It is also true that, so far, pragmatists have, as a rule, not gone far beyond Dewey's general recommendations and early educational reforms, both in point of method and systematic exploration. As regards logical positivism, while its contributions are not to be underestimated, it has so far fallen short of even imagining the uses to which a perfected analysis of meaning could be put. Some of its proponents have claimed no greater victories than the slaying of an already quite dead and barely breathing "metaphysics", an animal which, surviving metaphysicians claim, may not even have existed in the form in which it was feared and rendered "meaningless". Even the popularizers of positivism, the semanticists, could conceive of no greater philosophical challenge than language-therapy. In view of both the pervasiveness and importance of communication there is no ridiculing their campaign. But there is also nothing very satisfying about leaving it at that.

Remains Neo-Kantianism. To the extent that it was not stopped cold in Germany, it made its most distinctive contributions either by way of methodological explorations or, in Cassirer, its most brilliant representative, by way of the suggestion of a philosophical system so comprehensive in nature that it has so far been difficult to give it the attention it requires and thus to assign to it the significance which it may or may not merit. It is the purpose of the present book to overcome this difficulty by attempting to examine Cassirer's *Philosophy of Symbolic Forms* more closely than has so far been done.

2

Twice during the last fifteen years did scholars, of many callings and countries, collaborate and, by *Festschrift* and commemorative volume, express their appreciation of the work of ERNST CASSIRER. Since the turn of the century, in many languages and more than a hundred books, essays and articles, the thought of this great among contemporary philosophers has ranged from compendious historical investigations into the "problem of knowledge", interpretations of culture-periods, philosophers, scientists, poets to penetrating analyses of mathematics, physics, chemistry, psychology, history, linguistics and mythology. Yet, while Cassirer achieved early fame with well-documented presentations of other men's ideas, his own philosophy was not developed before the publication of his *Philosophie der Symbolischen Formen*, the latest volume of which appeared in 1929, at a time when in Germany phenomenology and the "Lebens-philosophischen" precursors of existentialism had all but eclipsed the classicism of Cassirer's theme and style. His philosophy proper could, therefore, neither receive the attention which a German intelligentsia gave to lesser intellectual events in the anxious pre-Hitler days; nor could an English-language audience, lacking a complete translation of his principal work, satisfy the interest in his thought which some of his (translated) books had already provoked.

We thus face the not unfamiliar paradox that a lively interest in his philosophy goes hand in hand with just as lively an uncertainty as to what this philosophy is about. To be sure, prior to the complete publication of his *Philosophy of Symbolic Forms* in English[1], it will neither be possible to give to Cassirer's thought the attention which it deserves, nor to assign to it the importance which it may possess. In the meantime, and to encourage such an enterprise, there may be some value in examining the basic orientation of his work more closely than has so far been done.

Since Cassirer's ideas on scientific concept-formation, language, myth, history, etc., are by now available in such translated works as *Substance and Function* [2], *Essay on Man* [3], *Myth of the State* [4], *Language and Myth* [5], *Rousseau Kant, Goethe* [6], and *The Problem of Knowledge* [7], I have not confined myself in the following pages to the selective treatment of any one of these particular aspects or applications of his philosophy. Instead, I have attempted to examine, in the symbolic-form concept, the core-idea upon whose proper understanding hinges whatever evaluation will in the end be made of Cassirer's contribution to philosophy.

In focussing upon the symbolic-form concept, the unpleasant alternatives had to be faced of either keeping the discussion on a level of such generality that its relevance for specific contexts would remain obscure, or missing the dominant theme by giving too detailed an account of the many realms of its application. Attempting to avoid either extreme, it is my hope that references to historical, scientific, mythological and linguistic subject-matter have been sufficient at least for the purpose of appreciating its bearing upon the significance of the symbolic-form concept. This could not have been done, however, without touching upon issues of which a more thorough treatment, while desirable, was necessarily beyond the competency of one inquirer. Only summary attention was therefore given to many topics which had to be of secondary importance for a study whose primary purpose was not to achieve definitive correctness with respect to the rich cargo of subject-matter considered by Cassirer, but rather to focus on the "Symbol-concept" for which all these topics are offered as providing so many different types of exemplification.

The exposition and discussion of the symbol-concept (Ch. III, IV) is flanked by four chapters; two historical ones (Ch. I, II) looking back to traditional philosophy; and two terminal ones, (Ch. VI, VII) taking issue with more recent types of sign-analysis. Cassirer himself has been wary of the fashion of interpreting ideas in isolation from their problem-contexts. Yet, while he was masterful in clarifying the thoughts of other thinkers in their historical interconnections, his own thought, aside from rather frequent references to Kant, is presented to us without the benefit of having its features contrasted with both traditional and contemporary schools of thought. I have, accordingly, started out by way of an historical approach. In the first chapter, I have examined a number of familiar figures in the history of philosophy for the purposes of: *a*) indicating their characteristically different evaluations of the "symbolisms" of word and number for knowledge of the "real"; and, *b*) clarifying, by an analysis of how this tradition looks if viewed from the vantage-point of a philosophy of symbolic forms, the shift in perspective typical for both Cassirer's approach and method of dealing with some of the pervasive problems of this tradition. Kant's philosophy has been considered with some attention, since it is within its epistemological provisions that Cassirer's own work has developed.

Finally, I have sought to contrast the implications of a theory of symbolic forms for semantics and pragmatics with the type of sign-analysis currently carried on under the title of "semiotic".

My expository, critical and historical approaches at best may help to make intelligible both meaning and import of Cassirer's general thesis. At worst, they may have touched upon more issues than could have been illuminated within my given space and means. But while these pages will be of different value to different readers, it is my hope that they may assist those who, already familiar with some of Cassirer's writings, will find that this presentation has made more amenable for clarifying discussion his symbol (symbolic form-) concept, upon whose proper understanding must depend any adequate evaluation of Cassirer's contribution to philosophy.

CHAPTER I

SYMBOL, REALITY AND THE HISTORY
OF PHILOSOPHY

The contemporary vogue of putting one's ideas into "empty space", without inquiring into their connection with the philosophical enterprises as a whole, never seemed a commendable procedure to Cassirer. Yet, while as an historian of philosophy, he has been careful to make clear the problem-context of the thinkers and systems he so successfully interprets, his *Philosophy of Symbolic Forms* has come to us without the benefit of having its relationship to other philosophical schools of thought clearly indicated.

As regards related contemporary efforts, Cassirer had planned to examine areas of agreement and divergence in a book that was to be entitled *Leben und Geist; Zur Kritik der Philosophie der Gegenwart* [1]. Unfortunately, it remained unwritten. With respect to the relation of his work to his "predecessors", however, while there is no systematic account by his own hand, historical references occur so frequently throughout his work that these may, without much risk, be integrated in such a manner that it will become quite clear how "traditional philosophy" must appear if looked at from the vantage point of his *Philosophy of Symbolic Forms*.

In what follows, only the outlines of such an historical reconstruction will be attempted. There is no purpose to such an excursion except to make a first, if indirect, approach to the central concern of Cassirer's philosophy, by noting what would "happen" to a number of selected figures in the history of philosophy if viewed from a different and highly original perspective.

Now just what sort of clarification may one expect from such "historical confrontations"? It is characteristic of all major philosophical traditions that each one, from the vantage point it reaches, gains a new view of the preceding stages of speculation.

The idea suggests itself that this conscious urge for self-justification may be one of the defining traits of philosophy. Each original philosopher would appear to be writing – if only by suggestion – his own "history" of philosophy. Thus, when Plato reflects on what philosophy had been previous to Socrates, he finds that philosophers "... talked to us in a rather light and easy strain ... as if we had been children, to whom they repeated each his story ... of one, two or more elements, which are or have become or are becoming..." [2]. For Plato there is a "mythical" stage of explanation preceding the stage of sophistication at which "Being" becomes a problem and the concept of its true nature is reserved to dialectical philosophizing.

Another, somewhat more explicit though also still sketchy "history" may be read from Book I of Aristotle's *Metaphysics*, where, in the light of his elaboration of the four causes, all previous philosophies are recounted as groping and incomplete attempts in the right direction. "Our review of those who have spoken about first principles and reality and the way in which they have spoken, has been concise and summary; but yet we have learned this much from them, that of those who speak about principles and cause, no one has mentioned any principle except those which have been distinguished in our work on nature. But all evidently have some inkling of them, though only vaguely" [3]. "History" of philosophy would accordingly fall into the two phases of partial and complete realization of the final and effective system of explanation with the latter superseding the former in the more thorough and circumspect analysis of the principles most of which had been singly realized by pre-Aristotelians.

Even such comparatively unhistorical thinkers as Bacon and Descartes find it impossible to argue for their "revolutionary" views in isolation from repeated contrast-references to what they conceived as the "barrenness" of Aristotelian scholasticism. In this vein, histories of philosophy could be, and have been, written in which the record of philosophical attainments is told in terms of a productive, empirical period on one hand and a syllogistic, metaphysical history on the other. Thus Kant's manner of viewing all pre-critical philosophy as running in the two streams of rationalism and empiricism has become the very framework in which scores of "histories of philosophy" were conceived. More recently, the pragmatic doctrine has inspired still different versions of how all "traditional" philosophy is to be understood, with the fundamental dichotomy of "static" and "dynamic" conceptions of reality as the principle of division [4].

While such a brief survey is certainly not much evidence for anything in particular, it may at least suggest that there is a general frame of historical reference implicit in most, if not all, philosophical traditions. If so, it may be asked, how does this circumstance reflect on the validity of philosophical histories on one hand, and on the support philosophic positions may derive from historical considerations on the other?

As regards the first question, one may agree that each historical interpretation is not necessarily superseded because the philosophical position on which it hinges gives way to another dominant systematic perspective. An historical account is not automatically rendered groundless because the position (which it was designed to support) is subsequently given up. Thus Hegel's philosophical history of philosophy remains significant even for the non-Hegelian. Metaphorically speaking, one could say that all such "histories" throw broad beams of (colored) light into the philosophical past and that, while affording no final or detailed acquaintance with what they touch, they give away their particular position by the areas which they leave dark.

As regards the second question, namely what possible support "histories" may give to the persuasive force of a "system" if we have to accept the "system" prior even to comprehending its implicit historical interpretation of the past: if we assume that each philosophy has its own way of writing its history, must we not also asume that there are, in principle, as many such histories as there are possible systematic positions? And if this is so, what use can there be for the numerous historical excursions by which philosophers since ancient days have sought to enforce their arguments? Such fixed and partial glances over the historical past, instead of providing evidence *for*, would rather presuppose the evidence *of*, the general position from which they are taken. This entire argument is deceptive, however, unless qualified. What is important here is to realize that while it is

indeed essential to *understand* a particular philosophy in order
to make sense of its historical interpretation of the past, one is
not required to *accept* its position to appreciate the historical
evaluations that are derived from it; nor must one accept such
evaluations merely because one appreciates the systematic position from which they issue. There need be no contradiction in
sharing, e.g., Dewey's general philosophic position and at the
same time finding fault with the historical acumen of pragmatists
or, vice versa, in sharing Dewey's polemics against certain historical "schools of thought" without thereby being committed
to an acceptance of his "solution" to their problems.

The upshot of these preliminary remarks: historical references,
while unintelligible in isolation from the systematic perspective
within which they are made, do not, on the other hand, provide
historical evidence and support for that perspective.

With this in mind, it will not make sense to argue, in what
follows, *for* the "philosophy of symbolic forms" by contrasting
it with the background of the philosophic tradition. By discovering, however, how this tradition looks if viewed from the position
of a "philosophy of symbolic forms", we may hope to realize the
shift in perspective that is characteristic of Cassirer's approach
to and method of dealing with the traditional, as well as some
more recent philosophical issues.

While formal considerations would seem to demand that one
deal with the "system" before examining whatever historical
interpretation it involves, I have thought it advisable, for purposes of exposition, to make a first, if indirect, approach to
Cassirer's philosophy by examining how both the rationalistic
and empiricist evaluations of "symbols" set the problem for
which he attempts to provide an acceptable answer.

I have suggested that each characteristically new way of
philosophizing provided a different principle of division by which
its achievements could be understood in contrast to all previous
inquiries. For the Platonist, the line may be drawn between the
"theorist" of ideas on one side, and all the earlier cosmologists
and physiologists on the other; for the Aristotelian, there are
only "groping" predecessors as partial contributors to the final
philosophy, while still others (Vico, Hegel, Comte) provide for
more than one stage preceding their own "culminations" in

philosophy. Our question now is: what is the principle of division
for Cassirer's conception of philosophy as distinguished from
traditional philosophy? From a thinker of Cassirer's historical
acumen it can not be expected that continuities will be neglected
or hard and fast lines of separation drawn. Cassirer is not under
the illusion of offering either a brand-new method of philosophizing or entirely new subject-matter not hitherto disclosed. But
he is aware of the distinctive scope and import of his conception
of philosophy as a theory and critique of symbolic forms.

A safe way, because a most general one, of stating this crucial
difference would be to say that, for Cassirer, all philosophy has
been the ever repeated attempt to get beyond the pictorial and
discursive symbolisms of language, art and the sciences to a
direct apprehension of the "Real" as such. With respect to this
objective, "the entire history of philosophy, regardless of all its
inner systematic differences, unaffected by all the strife of its
schools, seems to move in the same direction. Philosophy is
constituted in this act of self-assertion, in considering itself
confidently as the organon of knowing the real. In this sense the
maintenance of an "adequatio rei et intellectu" remains its natural point of departure" [5].

Now, if this distinction is kept on such a high level of generality,
it becomes indeed a secondary consideration whether a philosophy is symbol-conscious or not, whether it trusts the symbolisms of knowledge or art to bring man into contact with "Being",
or whether it bids us to forego reliance on them, in order to
appreciate the "Real" in the unmediated contacts of perception,
intuition or inspiration. Where common-sense, the arts, religion,
and even the sciences, can grant only partial perspectives, if
not "subjective" distortions, it is the philosopher who would
seem to be offering the "whole truth" about "being as such".
Whether we consider Parmenides' rationalistic identification
of "being" and "thought", or Berkeley's "esse-percipi" formulation, in either case we are offered an "identity"- equation between "being" on one hand and the respective philosophical
faculty par excellence on the other. Rationalist as well as empiricist schools of thought, regardless of all other differences
between them, would, from this general point of view, be fired by
the same drive: to disclose to the philosopher the naked truth,

to draw aside the veil of Maya, woven by the symbols of man's limited power of articulation, and to provide methods by which, stepwise or all at once, by constructively using symbols, or after distrustingly casting them aside, either a foothold or an outlook upon the "really real" may be reached. If this is the philosophic temper, then the actual and culturally given forms in which we symbolically represent, talk or think about "reality" will appear to it as so many limited aspects of human activity which stand in need of being "grounded" upon an "underlying" reality. Religions, arts and the sciences will be interpreted as media by which that "reality" is not so much revealed as rather characteristically distorted. It is the distinctive trait of Cassirer's philosophy of symbolic forms to have questioned this assumption basic to both pre-Kantian empiricism and rationalism. Instead of being engaged in the heroic pursuit of a "being" and a "truth" prior to, or beyond the limitations of, the symbolic media of the languages of myth, the arts, commonsense or the sciences, Cassirer considers it the very task of his "philosophy of symbolic forms" that it should specify for each of the symbolic media (beyond which there is neither being nor truth for man) its characteristic "index of refraction".

In subsequent chapters, the epistemological status and the modalities of these "symbolic forms", their relation to reality (and thus the type of metaphysics made possible by their application to traditional philosophical problems) will be dealt with more fully. In this chapter I shall substantiate the just-formulated contrast between the traditional and Cassirer's version of philosophy by considering a bit more closely the rationalistic and the empiricistic evaluations of symbolic forms in their quest for the "real".

HERAKLEITOS-PLATO-ARISTOTLE-DESCARTES-LEIBNIZ

If one were to frame a minimum definition of the schools of thought commonly referred to as "rationalistic", it would be possible to point to: 1) their implicit trust that the real (respectively "the truth about the real") may be reached at the end of a search which, either exclusively or in part, must employ symbols; and 2) their insistence upon either a specially refined *linguistic* (conceptual) symbolism, or some other symbol-system, such as is exhibited, e.g., by the *mathematical* disciplines. A mere "trust" in the power of verbal symbols would define not the platform of rationalism but rather of myth which conceives of "all verbal structures as also mythical entities, endowed with certain mythical powers, (so) that the word, in fact, becomes a sort of primary force in which all being and doing originate" [6]. A study of Herakleitos' fragments is rewarding in this connection. As we read his epigrammatic statements on words and speech (logos), we move as in a twilight zone between myth and philosophy. Hand in hand with a mythical power-interpretation of the "logos" (as the "steerer of the universe"), there is suggested the idea of an order quite beyond the personal capriciousness of the gods: "The sun may not transgress its measured course..." (fragment 94). What we called the "rationalistic equation" is manifest in Herakleitos' trust that the order of the logos, while eternal and indestructible, reveals itself nevertheless quite unmistakably in both the realms of nature and language. In other words: final insight into the cosmic process, if difficult, is yet possible and it consists in realizing the intelligence that works through everything. (fragment 41). Strangely enough, this identity between *logos* and *physis* is neither weakened nor upset by what has often been referred to as his proverbial obscurity. Take such fragments as: "Fire lives the death of earth and air lives the fire's death" (72) or "It is always the same, that is: living and dead, waking and sleeping, young and old. For this, through change, becomes that, and that, through change, becomes this". (88).

Passages such as the above would seem to render questionable what we called Herakleitos' "trust in language". In the light of other fragments, however, it is suggested that they be read as a protest against just one particular mode of linguistic usage rather than against the limitations of language as such. If, as Herakleitos admonishes us throughout, it is wisdom to look upon the logos as "what all things have in common" [2], then it would indeed be foolishness to believe that one may hope to grasp it either in the particularity of the word or in the separateness and isolation in which our senses grasp and distort it. Just as Herakleitos looks upon the many things, of which our "ears and eyes tell us poorly', as engulfed in the ceaseless flux of becoming in which they are both destroyed and conserved, just so the particularization of meaning, effected by the "word", is to be overcome, destroyed and conserved in the larger context of "speech" as a whole. The ambiguity, characteristic of words if taken out of the context of the linguistic flux, would appear not so much as an incurable shortcoming as rather a typical moment of their expressive powers. There is, in other words, no other limitation to the word than that exhibited throughout by nature herself. As fluid, not rigid, determinations, words illustrate perfectly the basic dialectic within which the logos must be sought. Whatever appear, to our senses, as opposites, are expressed, in language, as contradictions. For Herakleitos there is no other way by which language can render the true structure of being except by becoming itself engaged in the interplay of diction and contradiction, thus reflecting, on the level of speech, the interplay of position and opposition, the flux of coming about and ceasing to be which characterize the logos both of nature and speech.

Turning now to the Platonic dialogues and considering merely the relation suggested by them between "symbolisms" (verbal or mathematical) on the one hand and "true being" on the other, we discover a new sophistication with respect to the qualifications now demanded from valid types of symbolisms. Plato, like Herakleitos, expresses both trust in and distrust of the possibilities of language. We read from the dialogues both a rejection of the linguistic symbolisms of commonsense-language (exploited by the Sophists), and also a basic confidence that by means of auditory and visual symbols, which mediate discourse, one may be led up to the stage at which the true reality of the ideas becomes intuitable. The philosophic exercise proper would be, in this classic view, the untiring attempt to transform the word-symbolism of commonsense into the conceptual symbolism of well-defined discourse. The operator of this transformation would, of course, be the "expert of asking and answering questions", i.e., the dialectician whose task it is to determine "if the names are (to be) rightly given". (*Cratylos*, 390). The Platonic dialogues, whatever else they have been interpreted to mean, may, from the angle of our question, be taken as so many illustrations of a method by which the indefinite linguistic symbols employed by the Sophists are translated into the more rigidly defined symbols constructed by the dialectician. The method used in this translation has been sometines called an "inductive" one, presumably in view of the fact that Socrates is reported to have started with, and to have gone through, many instances of common sense meanings before attempting to define them in the light of implicit logical standards; it has been someties alluded to as "analytic", probably in recognition of the fact that Socrates, having reached defined concepts, does not claim them as (subjectively or objectively) new findings but rather as having somehow been implied in the minds of the discursing parties (Socrates as "midwife"). Plato himself referred to his method as a "carving art" (*Phaedros*, 265 A; Aristotle: *Politics* I, 1), a method of "division" and "unification", analysis and synthesis as which it impressed Galileo in particular. To refer to the method as "dialectic" has the advantage of indicating the symbolic medium in which the final "theoria" is actually achieved, i.e., in "discourse". This term, however, must be kept wide enough to accomodate definition-conscious language as well as the telling of myths, – both necessary symbolic vehicles for the understanding and final vision of the "Good" as the "idea of order". There are yet other symbolisms which the dialectician must master, those of "number" and "figure" because "he has to rise out of the sea of change and lay hold of true being, and therefore he must be an arithmetician". (*Republic* VII, 525).

Thus, while it is still the ideas that are real, and not any of the however well-defined symbolisms of either discourse or mathematics, a relationship of "metechis" is suggested for these latter as well as for all other sensuous "paradigmata" through which we are led to grasp the ideas. Adopting a more contemporary idiom, we could say that the Platonic dialogues exhibit not only a rejection of an undefined in favor of a defined discursive symbolism, but also that in the appreciation of the latter, they imply a clear distinction between the symbols, as the sense-embodied "vehicles" or "tokens" of the ideas, and the "meaning" of the discursive and mathematical symbolisms themselves which are elucidated by the art of the dialectician.

With modifications, characteristic of their different intentions, Aristotle, Descartes and Leibniz would seem to toe the Platonic line on these two points: (*a*) the rejection of certain types of symbolisms (namely those having their referents in commonsense, sense-impressions or unexamined tradition), and (*b*) the implicit trust in some privileged symbolisms, such as are exhibited in the formal relations elaborated by grammar, arithmetic, geometry and the various languages of method in which both criteria of certainty and procedures of valid derivation are indicated.

As regards Aristotle, for example, it has become almost commonplace (since Trendelenburg's: *Geschichte der Kategorienlehre*, 1846) to point to the structure of the Greek language as the schema from which his doctrine of the categories appears to have been drawn. Cassirer, who originally accepted this interpretation[7] has more recently qualified his view. In an article on *"The Influence of Language upon the Development of Scientific Thought"* he recalls that Aristotle was after all "not only a logician; he was at the same time an acute and accurate observer of natural phenomena. In order to do justice to his system of physics, we must pay heed both to the empirical and the speculative sides of the problem" [8]. Even on this more judicious interpretation, however, a connection between the Aristotelian concept of being and the general function of the symbolism of language is too obvious to be denied. To achieve his classification of natural phenomena, "Aristotle refers and appeals to those classifications that, before the beginnings of an empirical science of nature, have been made by language. Language is not possible without the use of general words – and these names are not only conventional signs; they are supposed to be the expressions of objective differences. They correspond to different classes and properties of things. He thinks that the words of language have not only a verbal but also an ontological meaning. Arguing upon this principle, we may say that there is a double approach to ontology, to a general theory of being. We may begin with an analysis of the fundamental phenomena of nature; but we may also begin just as much with an analysis of the linguistic phenomena – we may study the general structure of the sentence. In both cases we shall be led to the same result" [9].

Regardless then which of the two approaches is taken as the schema for the other, this much may perhaps safely be stated: Aristotle's categories, naming the most pervasive traits of being, at the same time also function as the most universal types of assertion. While, considered ontologically, they are taken to list the predicates of being on a level of highest generality, they may be developed both from an analysis of being and from an analysis of the ways of our "speaking about being".

A more detailed study of this problem would have to pay special attention to the difference between what, for Aristotle, are the *conventional* symbols of "voces" and "litterae" and of such *"natural symbols"* as are basic to all knowledge and the objects of immediate knowledge themselves. (*Posterior Analytics*, I, 3) "Natural symbols", as has been pointed out by W. A. Wick, are revealed by a "complete reflexive intuition of the intellect by which we are said to know immediately that we know immediately and which reveals that the nature of the intellect is merely that of the objects which it mirrors, so that concept and reality are formally identical" [10]. It must be remembered, however, that even these "natural signs" – as the originative source of science reveal a universal, i.e., "man", not "Callias", and therefore must be expressible within the symbolism of language. (*Posterior Analytics*, XIX, 15).

Indirect evidence for the decisive role of linguistic considerations within the Aristotelian system may be read from the close connection in which logical and grammatical investigations were carried on by the medieval Aristotelians, as well as from the attacks by which such thinkers as Valla, Vives and Ramus later attempted to undermine its alleged universality by disclosing its dependence upon purely linguistic considerations. (Cassirer: *Das Erkenntnisproblem*. I, p. 120).

The Renaissance battle-cry against the "barbarism" of Aristotle's metaphysics seems to have been sounded in connection with the demand to get away from preoccupations with "names– in order to become more closely acquainted with the phenomena of "nature". In Cassirer's studies in the philosophy of the Renaissance, however, (*Individuum und Kosmos in der Philosophie der Renaissance*, 1925) evidence is mustered for a somewhat different interpretation according to which the 13th- and 14th-century attacks against the "systems" of the schoolmen express not so much a demand to dispense with (symbolic) language in favor of a more immediate contact with nature, as rather so many proposals to substitute for the conventionalities and artificialities of language other, more precise, symbolisms, of the kind that were elaborated by the artists and mathematicians of that time.

If we examine, in this connection, Descartes' doctrine, in which this Renaissance-ideal of knowledge found its most influential philosophic foundation, its basic commitment to the "rationalistic equation" is easily recognized. Descartes, too, combines a rejection of the commonsense symbolism of ordinary language with an implicit trust in the symbol-systems of both a "mathesis universalis" and a "lingua universalis". As regards the "mathesis universalis", it must be so construed as to take account of those symbolisms which, to Descartes, "semblaient devoir contribuer que quelchose à mon dessein", i.e., logic, geometry and arithmetic. That this combination of disciplines did not amount merely to an unqualified acceptance of them issues clearly from (Part II of) the *Discours de la Méthode*. There both "l'analyse des anciens" and "l'algèbre des modernes" are charged with exercising the understanding at the cost of fatiguing the imagination. What is retained of Aristotelian logic, on the other hand, is not so much its specific rules of the syllogistic moods and figures but rather its methodological stipulations concerning the evidential status of the assertions from which one may start, as well as the permissibility of the steps by which one may deductively progress, in the pursuit of knowledge.

It is not to our purpose here to examine the specific modifications which both mathematics and logic would have to undergo if they were to make possible Descartes' "universal science" of order and relations. What is noteworthy for our task is merely to realize that he did trust its symbolism to apply universally to all things whatever. We know from the *Regulae*, how the application of Descartes' method prescribes a "reductio" of all sensuous properties to an estimation of a "more or less" which, in turn, requires precision by a number system, and how the assignment of numerical constants is again limited to what is spatially representable. What is maintained, in consequence, is that all the manifold configurations of reality reported by our senses become amenable to knowledge only to the extent that we succeed in translating them into relations obtaining within the "extended" which alone can be the referent for the symbol-systems of geometry and arithmetic.

One could ask at this point what such "translatability" may mean here. Descartes himself is quite clear in his rejection of a Platonic two-realm view. His "mathesis" is not to add new entities to the already familiar ones: "Cum enim hic nullius novi entis cognitionem expectemus, sed velim dumtaxat proportiones quantumque involutas eo reducere.." (*Regulae,* XIV).

No analogy, in other words, is being suggested between two levels of being such that one is held to resemble (pictorially or comparatively) the structure of the other. Occasionally, Descartes contrasts his method of expressing phenomena, too small to be observable, in terms of relations for which an intuitive geometrical reconstruction is possible, with the method of the scholastics who employed analogies in order to compare the most disparate species with each other. To speak, as we did above, of Descartes' method as effecting a "translation" from the sensuous properties of things into the symbolism of his "mathesis universalis" would, indeed, involve some mode of "analogy-thinking". A reminder of this sort would serve no purpose, however, unless different forms of analogical statements are distinguished. Thus, as Thomas Aquinas pointed out, a statement of the form "the lion is king of the beasts" is analogical in quite a different sense from the assertion that "two is to four as four is to eight". In the first example we compare states of affairs known antecedently; in the other, we grasp an "analogy by proportion", which, if properly interpreted, becomes a powerful instrument for the increase of knowledge.

Now it is surely a matter of definition whether only one, or both, of these modes of "analogy-thinking" are to be credited with affording "true" knowledge. There is no question, however, that for Descartes the greater precision possible through "analogies by proportion" determined the cognitive ideal of his "mathesis universalis". What we may know of things is accordingly not such of their properties as can be reported by our senses but only those relations into which they may enter as can be expressed by symbols put at our disposal by a science of magnitude and extension. "Non res ipsa e sensibus externis arunt proponenda, sed potius compendiosae illarum quaedum figurae" *Regulae,* XII). In a letter to Mersenne (November 20, 1629) Descartes makes mention of a "lingua universalis" which is to supplement his "mathesis universalis". The suggestion of such a universal symbolism of language – more comprehensive even than mathematical language – remained an ideal in the double sense of being considered by its author both possible and yet (at the time) unrealizable.

As a matter of principle, Descartes could well conceive of the possibility that by means of a limited number of linguistic signs and specifiable rules of combination an exhaustive description of all phenomena might be achieved, and would turn out to be just as valuable as the establishment of a system of arithmetic by number-signs and rules of operation had already proven to be. But the actual working out of such a gigantic plan as the "lingua universalis" presupposed the complete analysis of the entire content of human consciousness into its last constitutive, clear ideas. The successful completion of such a task, he felt, would have to wait until the application of his philosophic method had reached its final culmination. It is known that Leibniz took up this suggestion without sharing Descartes' cautious attitude about its early realization. In his remarks upon Descartes' above-quoted letter to Mersenne, he agrees that a perfected "lingua universalis" would depend upon the conclusions reached by a "true" philosophy [11]. In Leibniz' opinion, however, the accomplishment of such a philosophy need not precede the working out of a universal language. Both the analysis of ideas and the corresponding establishment of a sign-system should develop in close correlation. Leibniz' confidence (as against Descartes' caution) in this matter is perhaps rooted in the success he had experienced earlier with his "analysis of the infinite". The algorithm of the differential equation, he thought, had been proven not only as a convenient symbol of representing the results of mathematical reasoning, but as a true organon of increasing its scope. Analogously, an analysis of the fundamental signs that mediate all knowledge possible to the mind need not follow upon the analysis of ideas but may actually function as one of its most essential instruments.

There is perhaps a further reason why the postponement of a universal symbolism until after the establishment of a final system of philosophy could hardly make sense to Leibniz, who envisaged no finite end to the analysis of ideas anyhow. Not only do our perceptions stand in need of an ever-progressing analysis by means of distinct ideas, but in addition, our most abstract ideas themselves will always contain some "undistinguished" elements of perception. As Leibniz puts it in a reply to Bayle: "The most abstract thoughts are in need of some imagination; and when one considers the nature of these confused ideas (which never fail to accompany the most distinct ones of which we are capable) whether they be of color, odor or taste ... one recognizes that they always involve the infinite" [12]. Or: "Only geometrical knowledge and the analysis of the infinite have shown me the light and helped me to understand that our concepts also can be dissolved ad infinitum" [13].

One may wonder in this connection how this idea of an infinitely progressing analysis is to be harmonized with Leibniz' well-known dictum that to demonstrate the truth of an assertion it is only necessary to establish the meaning of the asserted predicate as implied by, or contained in, the connotation of the asserted subject-term. To be sure, Leibniz has given many illustrations of cases where such truth-demonstration can be achieved in a finite number of steps. But he also has mentioned others where no such definite demonstration can be performed. Thus, in the case of rational numbers, e.g., it is clear that any set of them can always be reduced to a common denominator or be reconstructed from this denominator in a finite series of operations. On the other hand, there are the irrational numbers which, incommensurable in the light of perfect reducibility, permit only of an ever closer approximation within the system of rational numbers. It is significant that for Leibniz the "phenomena of fact" also must be conceived as standing in this approximative relation to the "vérités de raison". What holds for the irrational numbers also holds for the "phenomena of fact". For assertions about them to be true it is accordingly not possible to demonstrate the predicate as implied *without residue* in the subject-term. It is merely required that a general rule of progression be indicated by means of which we are assured that any remaining amount of indistinctness will become gradually diminished. ("Quodsi appareat ex regula progressionis in resolvendo eo rem reduci, ut differentia inter ea quae coincidere debent, sit minus qualibet data, demonstratum erit propositionem esse veram") [14].

Keeping the above in mind, we could define the relation between our distinct ideas and the phenomena (which are known
through the symbols designating these ideas) by saying that this
relation is not to be understood in terms of an iconic correspondence as exemplified, e.g., between a sculpture and the person of
whom it is to be the likeness. As Leibniz puts it: "For a thing to
express another one, there must be a constant and ordered relation between what may be asserted of one and what may be
asserted of the other". (*To Arnauld*, Sep. 1687). For symbols to
designate phenomena it is sufficient that the relations formulated
by the former represent some relations obtaining among the
latter. Thus: "a model of a machine expresses this machine; a
plane, perspective drawing expresses a three-dimensional body;
a sentence expresses a thought; a sign expresses a number or an
algebraic equation expresses a circle; and what all these expressions have in common is that we may achieve by a consideration
of the (relations formulated in these symbolic) expressions, some
knowledge of the corresponding properties of the thing to be
expressed" [15].

In the light of these remarks, the demand for a "characteristica universalis" now becomes intelligible. If the analysis of
the infinite suggested to Leibniz the notion that the analysis of
our ideas may likewise not be exhaustible in a finite number of
steps, and if this realization in turn makes for a conception of the
relation obtaining between "ideas" and "phenomena" such that
the complexity of the latter could never be adequately expressed
(i.e., in all their relations) by a definite number of distinct ideas,
then we are indeed left with a purely symbolic mode of representation. At least some, and successively more, of these relations
would have to be comprehended by means of signs which would
stand for such distinct ideas as number, size, figure, motion,
solidity, etc. The "rapport" between the level of representation
and the level to which these representations symbolically refer
is established by Leibniz as *"naturel"*, as having a "fundamentum
in natura". If so, the epistemological possibility of successful
application of these symbols to phenomena is based upon Leibniz'
confidence in the "characteristica universalis" as a matter of
metaphysical presupposition.

For Leibniz the decisive question is not the possibility but the

potentiality of symbols, their usefulness for the edifice of knowledge. Symbolic characters are after all so much more easily
manipulated than phenomena, they are themselves "entities by
means of which relations obtaining among things may be expressed and with which we may operate more easily than with
things. To each operation with these 'characters' there corresponds an assertion about objects; often we may postpone our
dealing with these objects until we have come to the conclusions
of our operations. For every result obtained through the help of
the 'characters' may easily be transferred to their objects by
reason of the very correspondence which we have established between them from the start. The more precise these 'characters' are and the more relations between objects they designate,
the more useful they are".[16]

Yet, while the phenomena of nature never completely exhibit
the distinct features by which we "know" them within a symbol-
system as, e.g., geometry, "nevertheless the factual phenomena
of nature are, and must be, ordered in such a way that no actual
processes may ever violate the law of continuity ... or any other
of the rules of mathematics. Indeed, there is no other way to
comprehend things intellectually than by virtue of these rules
which ... together with those of harmony or perfection, furnished
by the true metaphysics, are alone capable of affording us insight into the reasons and motives of the creator of all things" [17].

This is not the place either to eulogize the modernity of this
view, or to challenge the "metaphysical" assumptions with which
it goes hand in hand. With respect to our central question this
much may perhaps be taken from what we have elicited so far:
the rationalistic equation has remained as intact for Leibniz as
for Plato some 2000 years earlier. There is agreement on at least
these points:

1) if knowledge of the real is to be possible at all within the
limitations characteristic of human beings, it can advance only
by means of certain privileged symbolisms (the sign-systems of
logic, arithmetic, geometry, mechanics, etc.).

2) while it is through these symbolisms that we must assure
ourselves of the structure of reality, we are merely led up by them
to the even more perfect stage of an immediate intuition of this
reality – either in rare moments of inspiration or, allegedly, in

the divine mind of the most perfect being.

3) symbolisms, designating clear and distinct ideas, do not stand in need of verification by the phenomena whose relational structure they express. The reality to which symbols refer is not the complex, vague and confused world of perceptions, but the order and relations of ideas with respect to which all actual relations and structures are but the "paradigmata". As Leibniz has it in the *Nouveaux Essais*: "The connection of the phenomena which guarantees factual truth with respect to the perceptual objects outside of us is verified by means of rational truths; just as the phenomena of Optics are illumined by Geometry" [18].

On the rationalist estimation of symbolic forms, we conclude, their "application" to the data of experience is of secondary importance and guaranteed by recourse to certain properties of the divinity. The primary contribution of the rationalists was the gradual success with which they managed to enlarge the scope of knowledge by an increasingly precise formulation of those linguistic and mathematical symbol-systems upon which depended the progressive analysis of complex ideas into combinations of distinct and well-defined ones.

LOCKE–BERKELEY

If again we leave out of our account all that is not directly relevant to our question, and if we focus on the empiricists' estimate of the office of symbols for the attainment of knowledge, we note that Locke, for example, seems in complete agreement with Leibniz' concern for a "thought-alphabet". The demand that an analysis of our knowledge into its distinct ideas be correlated with an examination of the meaning of linguistic signs is felt keenly by the author of the *Essay* who, in the third book, confesses; "When I first began this discourse of the understanding, and a good while after, I had not the least thought that any consideration of words was at all necessary to it. But when passing over the original and composition of our ideas, I began to examine the extent and certainty of our knowledge and I found it had so near a connection with words that, unless their force and manner of signification was first well observed, there could be very little said clearly and pertinently concerning knowledge"[19].

Once this relation between knowledge and language is properly appreciated, the examination of the "manner of signification" of words is held to supply the most evident support for the basic correctness of Locke's well-known analysis of knowledge. In order to get to the "original" of all our notions and knowledge, all we must do is to "remark how great a dependence our words have on common sensible ideas" [20].

The shift from the rationalist's type of sign-analysis is now indicated. There is, to be sure, a surface agreement between Locke and Leibniz: correct fixation of meaning by symbols is subsequent to examinations of distinct and simple ideas. But we must note that "idea" means different things to these two thinkers. To the Platonic, objective, logical meaning of the term there is now contrasted the modern, empirical, subjective, psychological connotation which we encounter in the first two books of Locke's *Essay*.

An analysis into the constitutive ideas to which symbols refer will, in consequence, discover "principles", if it is undertaken within the rationalistic scheme, and "contents of consciousness", compounded out of the elements of sensation and reflection, if undertaken within the empiricist scheme. There is a further difference which is crucial for our problem: for the rationalist, the validity of certain special symbolisms is guaranteed by virtue of the unquestioned presupposition that the distinct ideas designated by them are, or refer to, the "real". "La vérité étant une même chose avec l'être" [21]. The status of symbols becomes increasingly precarious, however, as soon as the implications of the empirical position are progressively developed. Once the rationalistic assumption is called into question, we are warned "not to suppose the words to stand also for the reality of things", on the grounds that "it is perverting the use of words, and brings unavoidable obscurity and confusion into their signification, whenever we make them stand for anything but those ideas we have in our minds" [22]. Once this stand is taken, we face the inescapable epistemological issue whether – and to what extent – the symbols by which we fix our own ideas, are bound to falsify, rather than to express, the nature of the things which we are to know by their mediation.

In his *Erkenntnisproblem* [23], Cassirer considered in detail the growing suspicion of a gulf between "words" and "reality" as typifying the empiricist movement from Hobbes' dictum "veritas in dictu non in re consistit" to Berkeley's hope for an "entire deliverance from the deception of words". As regards Locke, he still seems to strike a balance between the basic empirical conviction that all our ideas derive from particular occasions of sensation or reflection (save mathematical and moral ones which are intuited), on the one hand; and, on the other, the recognition that knowledge somehow involves elements of generality and thus requires expression through the generality of words. "It is not enough ... that sounds can be made signs of ideas, unless those signs can be so made use of as to comprehend several particular things; for the multiplication of words would have perplexed their use, had every particular thing need of a distinct name to be signified by". [24] As in his doctrine of substance and the primary qualities, the compromise he attempts here between an empirical commitment on one hand, and a recognition of the general character of language on the other, was a precarious one. Strictly speaking, there can be no "real existence" for Locke but in the particularity of "objects from which we receive our ideas" and the simple ideas which, as the "real existences", we "rank into sorts", designated by general names. Regardless of the use and advantage that Locke ascribes to the symbolism of language, it is not clear, within the system of knowledge outlined by him, how (verbal or other) signs could be said to designate either the particularity of "real objects" or the particularity of the simple ideas.

Berkeley, who seems to have made it his specialty to draw embarrassing consequences from Locke's "system of commonsense", did indeed come to this conclusion and, in consequence, denied the legitimate use of "general names". "We have shewn, I think, the impossibility of abstract ideas. We have considered what has been said of them by their ablest patrons, and endeavoured to show they are of no use for those ends to which they are thought necessary. And lastly, we have traced them to the source from whence they flow, which appears evidently to be language" [25].

The arguments by which Berkeley aimed to disclose the "impossibility" of abstract ideas do not concern us here; what matters is that their rejection implies also a denial that the symbolisms of language and mathematics, regardless of their practical values, can ever lead us to an understanding of the true nature of reality. A marked shift from Locke's attitude towards language is manifest.

Locke was convinced that an examination of the signs of language was instrumental and prior to a demonstration of the empirical thesis that all knowledge was ultimately based upon simple, "sensible" ideas. No such parallelism between language and knowledge is conceivable for Berkeley. According to his *Principles*, language is so far from illustrating the ways of knowing that it must be considered rather as its "most dangerous pitfall. In vain do we extend our view into the heavens and pry into the entrails of the earth, in vain do we consult the writings of learned men and trace the dark footsteps of antiquity; we need only draw the curtain of words to behold the fairest tree of knowledge, whose fruit is excellent and within the reach of our hand". (Par. 24).

It is well-known how this "tree of knowledge" metaphorically bears as its fruits our perceptions, which inform us of the "furniture of the earth". If all reality is to be lodged in the substantiality of the mind and its perceptions, and if it is the very characteristic of perceptions – in contradistinction from abstract ideas – to occur here and now, in the concreteness of their particularization, then it is clear that symbols, by virtue of their generality, cannot very well be expected to adequately denote reality at all.

A clear-cut decision, however, as to what exactly is the status of signs in Berkeley's thought is not quite so easy. Since we are concerned here less with the uniqueness of his system than with the empiricist's attitude towards symbols in general, we shall confine ourselves to indicating only briefly what seem to be essentially three distinct types of sign-functioning acknowledged by Berkeley: 1) The *linguistic* symbolism of words which commends itself for practical reasons even though it cannot put us in contact with reality. Communication is its pragmatic justification: "It cannot be denied that words are of excellent use, in that by their means all that stock of knowledge which has been purchased by the joint labors of inquisitive men of all ages . . . may be made the possession of one single person". (par. 21). Antedating the

more recent semiotic distinctions, Berkeley recognizes the informative and also the various emotive, prescriptive and appraisive symbol-usages: "There are other ends, as the raising of
some passion, the exciting to or deferring from an action, the
putting the mind in some particulardis position" (par. 20). 2) The
representative symbolism which governs not the relations
between signs on the one hand and our perceptions on the other,
but the very connections obtaining among our perceptions themselves. Thus, "the connection of ideas does not imply the relation
of cause and effect, but only of a mark or sign with the thing
signified". (par. 65) Fire, perceived through sight, is not the cause
of the perception of pain, but the perception of fire is the sign
that "forewarns" me of the perception of pain. Besides what is
given as immediate perception, we may also "perceive sensible
things mediately by sense, – that is, when from a frequently
perceived connection the immediate perception of ideas by one
sense *suggests* to the mind others, perhaps belonging to another
sense, which are wont to be connected with them" [26]. 3) The
theological symbolism, manifest in the *Siris*, according to which
our entire sensible world is presented as one gigantic symbolism.
What, on previous reflection, appeared as the "reality of our
perceptions" is interpreted, in the later work, as the sensuous
vehicle of a universal symbolic language through which the divine
spirit communicates itself to our finite minds. It is from this
vantage-point that Berkeley makes a belated contact with Plato
whom he now undertakes to defend against both Aristotelians
and Platonists alike [27].

Now as regards Berkeley's "theological symbolism", it surely
is not characteristic of the empirical tradition as a whole. With
respect to the verbal and representative types of symbolization
listed above, their family-resemblance with a more recent, be-
havioristically oriented semiotic is unmistakable. If viewed from
this position, these "signs" shine, if at all, with the light borrowed
from the perceptions which they "name" or "suggest". Contrasting Berkeley's view with Galileo's, for example, for whom perceptions share the illusory character of the mere "nomi" (verbal
signs), one cannot but realize the shift that now has come about.
What rationalists have traditionally branded as "illusions" for
Berkeley have become the sole guarantee of having reached the

indubitably real. And vice versa: the "letters" by which, according to Galileo, we are enabled to read the book of nature, appear in Berkeley's critique as instances of the "generality of names", – held incompetent in their abstractness to put us in touch with concrete reality to which perception alone holds the magic key.

It is in this preference for the self-evidence of perceptions over the mediacy of discourse and "abstract notions" (not "abstract ideas", – because these are strictly impossible for Berkeley) that Cassirer has seen the decisive departure of empiricists from a symbol-trusting rationalism [28]. In the light of the preceding considerations, a somewhat different interpretation may be preferable. Rationalism, while it has justly been understood as an attempt to push beyond the symbols of commonsense language to the "true order of reality", has done so by employing and trusting other types of symbol-systems, by which such "true order" could demonstrably be disclosed. Berkeley, on the other hand, while he has justly been said to have attempted to push beyond the symbols employed by both philosophers and scientists nevertheless assumed what we called a "representative symbolism" within which the perceptions themselves stand in relations of mutual signification to each other. For Berkeley "relations" are, after all, as obvious as "spirits" and "perceptions" [29]. In consequence we must allow that, for Berkeley, perceptions function both as the primary data of all knowledge and also as "signs" and "suggestions" for other perceptions. Instead of distinguishing, with Cassirer, a symbol-trusting rationalism from a symbol-rejecting empiricism, it would seem more judicious to recognize differently oriented symbolisms in the two cases.

Simplifying the issue somewhat, one could perhaps say that, while rationalistic symbolisms are most frequently drawn from logic and the mathematical sciences, empiricists have capitalized on evidence proper to associationist and introspective psychology. Thus, Berkeley is actually using psychological arguments in his attacks upon Newtonian physics [30], while a later empiricist, Ernst Mach, went so far as to attempt a reconstruction of mechanical physics in terms more consonant with the "facts" of psychology.

We have indicated areas of disagreement between the rationalistic and the empiricist evaluation of symbols and their office for the attainment of knowledge. It remains to state what, from the standpoint of Cassirer's philosophy of symbolic forms, are the common assumptions of these two schools of thought:

1) Both are illustrations of what have been called "nothing-but"-philosophies. They rely on privileged symbolisms for their grand tour to the "really real". For both, there is one, and only one, structure of Being; and it is disclosed, if not in the hierarchy of conceptual symbols, then in the connection of mutually signifying perceptions; if not in the symbols of number and figure, then in the languages of physiology and psychology.

2) Both are fired by the same cognitive ideal. Neither rationalists nor empiricists, regardless of all other distinctions between them, would be satisfied with merely offering us interpretations of aspects of reality. To be sure: once a "true structure of reality" is presupposed (be it biological, mechanical, mathematical or theological) it makes no sense any more to speak of a variety of (pragmatically justifiable) aspects, which would necessarily have to be evaluated as belonging to different levels of remove from what is assumed as expressive of the "true" features of Being. Instead of an *"interpretation"* of reality by symbols we meet in both schools of thought with the stipulation of an *"interpenetration"* of ideas (concepts, mathematical symbols or perceptions) on the one hand and reality or "true Being" on the other. In this sense, the common, unquestioned objective of both movements remains the "adequatio rei et intellectus". "The identity of subject and object, the absorption of one by the other, remains the genuine task of all knowledge, even when the conception of the means by which this goal is to be attained becomes radically modified. The interpretation may change, but there is no basic transmutation merely because "sensible perceptions" rather than "pure thought" are credited with the task of providing the bridge from one realm to the other" [31]. Whether, in this basic "equation", we substitute "perceptions" for "thought", no matter how different the constants we introduce, the form of the equation remains unchallenged. It is all the same basic conviction, whether we share Spinoza's belief that "as light illuminates itself and the dark around it" so our thought can reach a point at which both Being and Truth are self-evidently revealed, or whether we

follow Berkeley's advice to tear asunder the veil of words in order to lay hold, in primary perception, of reality at its most concrete.

It is at this point that Hume's "scepsis" set in. But while it is to Hume's credit to have disclosed convincingly the dogmatism of the equational assumption, it is the lasting merit of Kant to have subjected its "metaphysical" presuppositions to his critical analysis.

We shall try to show in a later chapter how Cassirer opposes to the "nothing-but" attitude of empiricism and rationalism the suggestion of a far greater variety of legitimate and fertile symbol-usages than the few privileged ones to which both dogmatic schools of thought had confined themselves. In this task Cassirer was encouraged by the advancing development and the increasing precision of the more recent symbolic systems of logic, non-Euclidean geometries, modern physics, psychology, linguistic, etc. We shall have to conclude that Cassirer's philosophy may best be understood as a conscious attempt to draw the philosophical consequences of both Kant's transcendental contribution and the contributions of modern science, in their bearing upon this basic problem of occidental philosophy: the symbolic nature of our knowledge of reality. Before proceeding to this account, we must consider which features of Kant's critical method would appear to be relevant for such a philosophy.

KANT

A recapitulation of Kant's epistemological doctrine is not necessary here, nor would it seem wise in the case of a philosopher about whose heritage both disciples and adversaries seem to singularly disagree. Even to recapitulate would be to take sides. As Lachelier was reported to have remarked to Léon Brunschvicg: "In France one has refuted Kant for some fifty years – without understanding him; for another fifty years one admires him now – without understanding him any better". In what follows we shall confine ourselves to comments upon a number of selected passages, which we think are indicative of what Cassirer takes to be Kant's "transcendental" contribution towards a more adequate formulation of the symbolic nature of knowledge, than was achieved either by rationalism or empiricism.

We mentioned above two basic assumptions upon which both schools appear to be agreed. We also indicated that it was with respect to one of these – the implicit belief that knowledge (conceptual or perceptual) could, at some point, make contact and become one with what is "truly real" – that Kant's "critique" will become relevant for our discussion. There is scarcely a book by Cassirer where reference is not made to Kant, crediting him with having replaced "coincidence"-, "copy"- or "correspondence"-theories of knowledge with what is interchangeably termed a "functional", "transcendental" or "categorial" interpretation of the problem of knowledge. It is this shift which is usually referred to as Kant's "Copernican revolution". Commentators have as a rule noted the misleading character of this comparison and pointed out that "whereas Copernicus deposed the observer from his geocentric primacy and rendered him much less important than he had been, the Critical Philosophy makes him more important than he had previously been supposed" [32]. That the analogy holds, however, in a different sense is clear once we consider that "in both hypotheses we find a drastic ... revision of a primary assumption which long had been allowed to pass unchallenged. In one case what is assumed is the immobility of the observer, in the other the passivity of the observer" [33].

Even in this formulation, however, the problem is merely touched upon, not really illuminated. As Cassirer remarks: "The Copernican revolution with which the *Critique* starts is neither understood nor appreciated if one sees in it a mere 'conversion' of the dependency-relation so far assumed between "subject" and "object", "knowledge" and its "object". In conceiving of such a turn-about, the elements whose mutual relation is at issue, would retain their original connotation, while it is the very meaning of the transcendental procedure that any modification of their mutual relationship would, at the same time, imply an essential modification of the meaning of these elements themselves" [34].

The notion of "objects", we are told, is to be replaced by taking note of the "modi cognoscendi" which alone account for whatever "objectivity" is attainable through their mediation. The shift referred to as Kant's "Copernican revolution" must therefore be understood in at least two senses. For one, it would refer to a substitution for the "adequatio rei et intellectus"-view of a functional one according to which reality, as the object of experience, is not so much "reached" as rather "conditioned" by the "constitutive" (intuitive and categorial) functions employed in cognition. Furthermore, this shift would indicate that a knowledge so defined could lay hold neither of such independent entities as Platonic ideas nor of the "esse" of Berkeley's perceptions but only of what Kant calls the "phenomena" or "objects of experience". Only of such "phenomena of experience" can it be said that they cannot be determined independently from the constitution of a "Verstand" and its synthetic *a priori* functions. „Only then can we say that we 'know the object' when we have effected synthetic unity among the manifold supplied by intuition" [35]. It is the task of the *"Analytik des Verstandes"* to understand this synthetizing effect as a whole and in its different forms. As the *Prolegomena* summarized: "The object itself remains forever unknown. But if, by means of the concept of the understanding, the connections between the representations through which (the object) is given in our sensibility, are universally determined, the object is thereby (also) determined and the judgment is objective". (Par. 19). In Cassirer's words: "To maintain the objective validity of an assertion does not imply a relation to a "something" confronting cognition as extraneous, but it is itself not possible except within the conditions imposed by that cognition" [36]. Hence, the transcendental method is required. Employing it, we must be "concerned not with objects but with our mode of knowing the objects" [37].

How this method is used in the deductions of the catagories, or how it is to be distinguished from an "empirical" one such as, for example, Locke's, will not concern us here. What matters for our discussion is that such a method would indeed be required once the assumption is made that "the unity of the objects is exclusively determined by the mind, i.e., according to conditions characteristic of the nature of the mind. Thus, the mind is the source of the general order of nature insofar as it comprehends all phenomena under its own laws ... Because we are not dealing with the nature of things "in themselves" (which depend upon the conditions imposed by our sensitivity as well as our understanding) but with nature as an object of possible experience" [38].

This somewhat strange assertion of the "mind" as the "de-miurge" of nature may not appear quite so paradoxical if one realizes that what Kant had in mind was not the assertion of any sort of a psychological or ontological "efficiency" of the "brain" through which it could impose what Herder once called a "Form-gebungsmanufactur" upon a chaotic reality. According to the "Marburg"-Kantians, the "demiurge"-metaphor merely refers to the basic presupposition of a formal (logical) relation between certain (categorial) schemes of determination, which, epistemo-logically, define the "mind" concept, and those features which we must conceive as constitutive of "objects of experience". Consider-able as Kant's "revolution" appears, if put this way, it may not impress one as quite so radical if one considers certain early sections of the *Kritik*. There, both "sensitivity" (Sinnlichkeit) and "mind" (Verstand) are referred to as two essentially distinct, contributive factors of knowledge. Sensitivity (which is called "Empfindung" as a modification of the subject, "Anschauung" when considered in relation to an object, and "Erscheinung" when considered as material for categorial determination) is sometimes taken as the medium through which "we are affected by objects", while it is the "mind" in which reside all the deter-minations that make for objectivity "ueberhaupt". Instead of a "Copernican revolution", we would seem to be faced here with an epistemological counter-part to Aristotle's "form-matter"-principle. Kant formulates indeed: "In a phenomenon, I call that which corresponds to sensitivity its matter; but that which causes the manifold of the phenomena to be perceived as arranged in a certain order, I call its form" [39]. "Matter" here designates the "undetermined per se", the "stuff" (formless by itself) to which all forms (of intuition and mind) must somehow become "added".

It is regarding this point, namely, how the "given" is to be understood in the context of Kant's critical enterprise, that a considerable variety of Kant-interpretations has arisen. On this issue, Cassirer (in the company of Liebert, Natorp, Hoenigs-wald and Bauch) goes along with Herman Cohen's contention that, strictly speaking, the "matter"-concept, designating the "given" as "affecting" the mind prior to and independent of the pure forms of intuition, cannot be made compatible with the rest of the Kantian critique. Such a view would indeed presuppose an illegitimate use of the phenomenally-restricted category of causality. In his *Erkenntnisproblem* [40], Cassirer charges Schopenhauer with having misread Kant in this fashion. As Cohen puts it in the characteristic heaviness of his style: "'Form' is correlative to 'matter'. Both are merely distinguished within the phenomenon. But the phenomenon, in the last analysis, is given in time, which is the form of all phenomena. Now: the phenomena, considered in abstraction from all form and law, stand for 'matter ueberhaupt' which likewise, as that to which the law applies, is itself a condition of knowledge. It is this conditional value (Bedingungswert) of matter, designated by time, which therefore is not improperly called the 'form of matter'" [41].

In his influential *Problem der Geltung* (The Validity-Problem) A. Liebert expresses the same thought: "Once one speaks of 'given-ness' (Gegebensein), once one even conceives of the mere notion of the given – then this is not anymore the 'merely given' in the sense of a knowledge-independent reality, but it is already a 'given-in-thought' (ein gedachtes Gegebensein)".

Cohen, who admits that there are 'unfortunate' ambiguities in the notion of the 'given' in the *Kritik*, refers his readers to the chapter called "Amphiboly of the Concepts of Reflexion" for Kantian formulations more consonant with the 'spirit' of his epistemology. In an examination of that chapter we find indeed that there the 'form-matter'-dichotomy is treated alongside such other pairs as 'Sameness and Difference', 'Agreement and Disagreement' and 'Inner and Outer'. This shift from the presentation of 'form and matter' as opposed ontological entities (Transcendental Aesthetics) to methodologically correlated distinctions of meaning, in the 'amphiboly'-chapter has appeared of special significance to the Marburg-Kantians.

Applying this interpretation to the "problem of perception", we may recall that in the *Prolegomena* Kant made a sharp distinction between 'judgments of perception' (Wahrnehmungsurteile) and 'judgments of experience' (Erfahrungsurteile); where the former claim only subjective validity ("I feel cold"), the latter alone can make 'objective' assertions ("It is 5 degrees below zero"). If read in the light of the 'amphiboly'-chapter, this radical distinction could now be interpreted as a relative and comparative one. All it could signify now would be the realization that "where our problem is to distinguish the world of our pre-scientific consciousness from the constructive determinations of scientific knowledge, perception may indeed be taken as something relatively simple and immediate. If considered with respect to the constructive determinations (of science) it may be taken as a mere 'datum', as something 'given'. But conceiving of it in this manner neither deprives us of the right nor indeed absolves us from the obligation to understand (perceptions), in different contexts, as something pervasively mediated and conditioned". [42].

How this interpretation opens the way for an extension of the transcendental analysis beyond the framework provided by Kant's *Kritik*, will be considered in the subsequent chapter.

Let us summarize now what, from the standpoint of a philosophy of symbolic forms, would appear to be the contribution as well as the limitation of Kant's theoretic philosophy. What light do the comments made so far on the meaning and implication of Kant's "Copernican revolution" throw upon the various symbol-interpretations of the predominantly rationalistic and empiricist thinkers? Of what merit is the proposed substitution of the "transcendental method" for the "adequatio rei et intellectus"-assumption basic to all pre-critical philosophy?

Since the status of symbols cannot be determined in independence from what we can know through their mediation, Kant's epistemological arguments against both the rationalist and empiricist versions of "knowledge" will apply also to their respective evaluations of symbols. Note that we are not concerned with the definitive correctness of Kant's thesis but only with the question of what follows for the status of symbols, as seen by pre-critical philosophers, if his arguments hold.

Supposing we formulate Kant's argument as follows: empiricists are committed to a concept of knowledge which would render incomprehensible the character of necessity peculiar to mathematics, whose successful employment for cognition is guaranteed by what Kant took to be the "fact of science". Rationalists, on the other hand, whose concept of reason could account for that character of necessity, have not furnished us with demonstrations that could make intelligible why their rational concepts and relations should so profitably apply to the world of sensuous experience.

Analogously we may say: the symbolisms of number and figure, definitory of the type of science Kant accepted as a fact, cannot be accounted for in terms of pre-critical empiricism. On the other hand, rationalism, which has been instrumental in developing these symbolisms and greatly trusts them as vehicles for an adequate expression of the true structure of reality, must assume a pre-established harmony (or "participation") which will guarantee application of the conceptual and mathematical symbol-systems to the experienced world of perception and becoming. Finally: rationalism has evidenced a consistent preference for symbolisms, such as mathematics and logic, which exhibit relations of necessity and universality only and, in consequence, could not accommodate (unless transformed, viz. Hegel's system) the symbolisms of such different character as are prevalent in experimental science, perception, art, myth and religion.

With the analogy drawn thus far, the bearing of Kant's critique upon an adequate conception of symbolic systems will now be clear. In Cassirer's words: "We must accept in all seriousness what Kant calls his 'Copernican revolution'. Instead of measuring the content, meaning and truth of intellectual forms by something extraneous which is supposed to be reproduced in them, we must find in these forms themselves the measure and criterion for their truth and intrinsic meaning. Instead of taking them as mere copies of something else, we must see in each of these symbolic forms a spontaneous law of generation, an original way and tendency of expression which is more than a mere record of something initially given in fixed categories of real existence" [43].

From this point of view, symbols are not to be taken as "mere figures which refer to some given reality by means of suggestion or allegorical renderings, but in the sense of forces, each of which produces and posits a world of its own. The question as to what reality is apart from these forms, and what are its independent attributes, becomes irrelevant here. For the mind only that can be visible which has some definite form; but every form of existence has its source in some peculiar way of seeing, some intellectual formulation and intuition of meaning" [44].

Now, whether such a reading of Kant's "contribution" is be-

lieved to be sound or not depends, of course, on the Kant-inter-
pretation one accepts. If one shares, for example, Russell's comments, Kant would, far from improving upon his predecessors,
be refutable by most of them [45]. If, on the other hand, the Mar-
burg-interpretation is found plausible, then Cassirer's application
of it to a more flexible philosophy of symbolic forms would also
be intelligible.

This brings us to a consideration of what, from the perspective
of this philosophy, would appear to be the limitations of Kant's
position. Cassirer commented on them first in his essay "Goethe
and Mathematical Physics" [46]. later in his studies on *Einstein's
Theory of Relativity*, and his introduction to the first and third
volumes of his *Philosophy of Symbolic Forms*. The gist of his
comments may be summarized this way: Kant has failed to
account for a great variety of synthesizing acts by which sensory
data may be "spelled out in order to be read as experiences".
By confining himself to an examination of the principles exhibited by Newtonian physics, Kant was lead to underestimate, if
not to miss totally, other significant structures present and
effective within "common experience" itself. If it is to be the
task of a transcendental method to understand all types of
"objectivation" (Gegenständlichkeit) as conditioned by specifiable acts of a synthesizing mind, then it should not have been
limited to the levels of the highest intellectual "sublimation" of
experience. Instead of restricting one's attention to the "super-
structure" of theoretical science, Cassirer recommends that the
philosopher proceed to tackle also the "sub-structure", i.e., the
various other domains of expression and representation in which
perceptions appear as so many ordered realms of "objectivation".
In support of this contention, Cassirer points to Kant's partiality
in treating of judgments of perception in a mere preparatory
manner, considering them just as "counterparts" to judgments
of experience. True, the concept of scientific experience requires
the presupposition of necessary relations pertaining to all experience. Consequently, perceptions too are subsumable under
the universal form-structure of both pure intuition and the
categories. In the *Kritik*, the chapter entitled "The Second
Postulate of all Empirical Thought in General" formulates indeed: "Whatever is connected with the material conditions of

experience (Perception) – that is real". But, one must ask here, what type of "connection" is actually considered by Kant? The answer is that he lists none but those which define the categories of which all natural (physical) laws are but so many specifications. To Kant, it is accordingly the same intellectual synthesis which makes both for the object of our common experience and for the objects of mathematical physics. In his own words: "Thus it is demonstrated that the synthesis of apprehension, which is empirical, must necessarily conform to the synthesis of apperception, which is intellectual and entirely a priori ... It is one and the same spontaneity which brings connection into the manifold of intuition, whether it is in the name of the imagination or in the name of the mind" [47].

Within the framework of Kant's philosophy perception can have only a quantitative significance. To characterize one perception in distinction from another would be merely to indicate, on some scale of magnitude, their respective places in a system of measurement. Kant's partiality to a merely intellectual signification of perceptions, his unquestioned reading of the principle of Euclidean geometry and Newtonian physics into the "forms" of intuition and mind, mark the important limitations of his system for a philosophy of symbolic forms.

What Cassirer never tires of attributing to Kant is his "Revolution der Denkart", according to which philosophers are freed from having to strain after a reality more profound (or more immediate) than the only one given in experience, as it is encountered or reflected upon by the methods of scientific synthesizing. Instead of undertaking, like ontological metaphysics, speculative inquiries into fixed traits of being, the transcendental method is praised for initiating an analysis of our intellectual functions, an examination of the types of judgments which logically condition whatever may validly be asserted as "objective". The "objectivity", however, dealt with by the *Critique of Pure Reason*, actually turns out to be an exclusively physical one. The transcendental method, as used there, has not provided us with a key for "objectivity as such" but specifially for just one type of objectivity, namely, the one that can be formulated within the set of principles constitutive of Newtonian physics.

In brief: what Cassirer accepts of Kant is his "transcendental method" which, unconcerned about immutable structures of being, inquires into the culturally given fact of science and "being not concerned with objects but with our mode of knowing objects" makes for a more flexible analysis of experience as consisting of so many different types of "synthesizing". In Cassirer's words: "The decisive question is always whether we attempt to understand function in terms of structure or vice versa ... The basic principle of all critical thinking, the principle of the primacy of the function before the object, assumes a new form in every discipline and requires new foundations" [48].

What Cassirer denies, on the other hand, is that Kant himself realized the full range of application for which his method could bear fruit. It is in this demand for an extension of Kant's critical method to domains of reality other than structured by science in general, and Newtonian physics in particular, that Cassirer's philosophy of symbolic forms will have to be examined.

CHAPTER II

REALITY AND SYMBOLIC FORMS

How, we must ask now, are both the pervasiveness and the objectifying office of the symbolic-form concept to be demonstrated? Keeping in mind Cassirer's Kantian orientation, it will follow that his inquiry into the objectifying pervasiveness of symbols cannot properly be expected to point to or to discover facts or activities hitherto unknown or inaccessible to either the sciences or such other culturally extant types of experience-accounting as religion, myth and the arts. Kant, it will be remembered, set out to clarify his "misunderstood" *Kritik* by showing in the *Prolegomena* that neither mathematics nor the physical sciences would be "possible" unless the pure forms of intuition and certain categoreal determinations were presupposed as valid for all experience. Analogously, Cassirer maintains that the symbol-concept must be taken as just as pervasive as are, in fact, the sciences, arts, myths and languages of commonsense, all of which he conceives to be employing symbols in their different experience-accountings.

To say, furthermore, that symbols "objectify" would, on this interpretation, mean nothing more than that these various domains themselves, in their symbolic evaluation of the perceptual data to which they apply, furnish the only contexts within which one can meaningfully speak of any kind of "objectivity". There is, in other words, no point in producing examples to illustrate exactly what Cassirer means when he credits symbols with "bringing about" rather than merely "indicating" objects, if only because all the sciences, arts, myths, etc., would have to be listed as illustrating this general contention. We must distinguish here two aspects of this contention: (1) That all the above-mentioned cultural "domains of objectivity" do indeed presuppose the employment of symbolic thinking, and (2) that there is no objectivity outside the contexts established by these various cultural domains.

As regards the last aspect, its acceptance follows from Cassirer's endorsement of what he took to be Kant's transcendental method. Could Kant prove the adequacy of this method by the use he made of it with respect to "experience as science?" The answer will be in the affirmative, if one keeps in mind the state of the mathematical and physical disciplines with which he was familiar. As A. P. Ushenko has put it: "In relation to his information Kant's intuition of Euclid's axioms is unobjectionable ... without the aid of Einstein's conception of a curved space, we should not conclude that Kant is altogether wrong" [1]. The answer may be in the negative if one considers that Kant presented his "forms" of intuition and understanding as immutable human faculties, taking them to be as *final* as Aristotelian logic, Euclidean geometry and Newtonian physics were thought to be *necessary*. But: whatever one's evaluation of Kant's position, this much of it is never questioned by Cassirer, namely, that the determinate form in which one experiences the "objective" world is never passively received *ab extra*, but rather is understandable, in principle, as conditioned by our acts of synthesizing the manifold given in sensation. What Kant had maintained was that there can be no objectivity in the physical sense without assuming the synthesizing forms laid down by the *Transcendental Analytic*.

This point is generalized by Cassirer to include domains other than physics, to be accounted for by types of synthesis other than those listed in the first *Kritik*. That aspect then of Cassirer's general contention, according to which there can be no objectivity outside the contexts established by the sciences, arts, languages and myths, instead of being explicitly demonstrated, constitutes his basic philosophical commitment to Kant's theoretic philosophy.

Regarding the other aspect of his thesis, namely, that all the contexts within which such objectivity is encountered, are to be understood as symbol-systems, insofar as all of them imply specific evaluations of the "same" sensory data, – on what evidence are we to accept it? Or better: what sort of evidence is possible for this contention, within the commitment to Kant's position? With respect to Kant's inquiry Cassirer maintains that the author of the *Kritik* aimed to develop the epistemological consequences of the sciences with which he was familiar. It was the actual employment by these sciences of "judgments" which were related to experience (synthetic) as well as necessary (a priori) that seemed to demand a revision of both the empiricist and rationalist pronouncements with respect to the nature of human knowledge. Considering the stage at which he analyzed it, Cassirer thinks that Kant's analysis was adequate for science as he knew it. Kant, in other words, was not concerned with adducing evidence that there *are* synthetic judgments a priori – the evidence for their actual employment being taken to issue from an impartial reading of the sciences themselves. It was but their "possibility" that, according to Kant, had to be accounted for by making those necessary presuppositions about human cognition, through whose mediation science, as a result of the activation of that cognition, would become intelligible. Consequently, these presuppositions, the forms of intuition and understanding, are not the evidence from which the synthetic a priori judgments of the scientist are thought to be derivable, but the sciences themselves are taken as the evidence that justifies the epistemological characterization of the "mind" with which the first *Kritik* is concerned.

This brief reminder serves to explain Cassirer's analogous conviction that his theory of the symbolically-mediate character of reality, far from standing in need of ingenious philosophical demonstrations, merely formulates, on a level of highest generality, a semiotic function which, in various modifications, is assumed as a matter of fact by all who, within the legitimate contexts of their respective branches of inquiry, investigate the nature of physical, artistic, religious and commonsense "objects". A re-examination of this evidence in the light of more recent developments in the mathematical, physical, psychological, linguistic, religious and anthropological researches considered by Cassirer, would both surpass the competency of any one inquirer and also be not to our immediate purpose.

For the remainder of this chapter our chief concern will be to explain how the symbol concept must be understood in order to warrant the universal use and significance which Cassirer attributes to it. Before proceeding to this task, however, let us note that, rightfully or not, Cassirer did take for granted its actual employment, not just in the analysis of the various disciplines, but in the very construction of the domains to which these analyses refer.

In support of this contention, consider the following: (1) Early in the first volume of his *Philosophie der Symbolischen Formen*, where Cassirer prepares for the introduction of the symbolic-form concept, he raises the question ". . . whether there is indeed for the manifold directions of the spirit . . . a mediating function and whether, if so, this function has any typical characteristics by which it can be known and described" [2]. Yet, although it is a foregone conclusion that such a "mediating function" must be ascribed to the symbol-concept, Cassirer, instead of presenting specific arguments for this core-idea, immediately goes on to say: "We go back for an answer to this question to the symbol-concept such as Heinrich Herz has postulated and characterized it from the point of view of physical knowledge" [3]. As soon as the question is raised, in other words, whether there is a function both more general and flexible than, for example, the concepts of "spirit" or "reason" (elaborated by traditional philosophy), the answer, in the form of the proposed symbol-concept, is not argued for at all but is presented as being actually effective and recognized as such by Herz with respect to physical science, and such other thinkers as Hilbert (mathematical logic), Humboldt (comparative linguistics), Helmholtz (physiological optics) and Herder (religion and poetry).

(2) In 1936 the Swedish philosopher Konrad Marc-Wogau had commented upon certain difficulties he found inherent in Cassirer's various versions of the symbol-concept. In a rejoinder to these objections, Cassirer makes this highly characteristic statement: "In his criticism, Marc-Wogau seems to have overlooked this one point, namely, that the reflections to which he objects are in no way founded upon purely speculative considerations, but that they are actually related to specific, concrete problems and to concrete matters of fact" [4]. It is significant that, here again, where the 'logic' of the symbol-concept has been challenged, Cassirer makes no attempt to take up his critic's suggestions on the same analytical level on which they were made but, instead, goes on to cite a variety of instances (drawn from psychology, linguistics, mathematics and physics) for which outstanding re-

Symbol and Reality

presentatives have already emphasized the symbolical character of their respective subject-matters.

Strange as this attitude may appear to those who would expect an original philosophy to develop and reason from its own axioms, it is only consistent in the light of the above-mentioned transcendental orientation in which Cassirer read and accepted Kant's philosophy. The basic thesis that the mind (*Bewusstsein, Geist*) is symbolically active in the construction of all its universes of perception and discourse is, accordingly, not suggested as a discovery to be made or to be grounded upon specifically "philosophical" arguments. Instead of presupposing insights different from, and requiring cognitive powers and techniques superior to, those which are accessible to empirical science, the thesis is developed as issuing from an impartial reading of the scientific evidence in all branches of investigation.

Certain difficulties about such a position may perhaps be felt from the outset. One may question, for example, whether scientific situations could be encountered at any time which would give univocal testimony to the symbolically-mediate character of both their methods and their subject-matter. One may also wonder whether scientific "crown-witnesses" (on whom Cassirer relies so heavily), when reflecting upon the symbolic nature of their domains, do so *qua* scientists, or whether, when so reflecting, they must be considered philosophical rather than scientific spokesmen for their disciplines. Finally, a philosophy which rests its case squarely on the evidence and success of not just one (especially "reliable") science but of all the sciences (including all religious and imaginative "sense-making" as within the province of what Cassirer calls "Kulturwissenschaften") would seem to be dangerously committed to generalizing upon enterprises notorious for their proneness to scrap both their own theories and the various attendant philosophical explanations of their theories.

Considerations of this type need not be fatal, however, to a philosophy thus far considered. A critical reading of the evidence of the sciences will indeed never face "univocal situations". Nor will such situations be encountered within any other inquiry. The cognitive enterprise, whether in the form of large philosophical generalizations, or of the more readily controlled scientific generalizations, is admittedly guided by hypotheses, and thus does imply decisions with respect to the type of data that are considered relevant for its respective generalizations. The further contention that the methodological *testimony* of the scientist cannot be credited with the same respectability as his methodological *effectiveness* also need not be damaging to a philosophy whose center of gravity is determined by the scientist's findings. Any philosophy, on the contrary, which is proposed as a critique of, and mediation between, the variously oriented symbolisms of knowledge must obviously do justice to the most reliably constructed symbol-systems of the sciences, and, in doing that, can hardly afford to disregard statements on method merely because they come from somebody who employs them successfully. At any rate, an adequate interpretation of the scientific symbolisms always requires attention to both the factual and the (methodo-)logical subject-matters, and there does not seem to be any *prima facie* evidence why the method-conscious scientist is to be trusted less in this connection than the science-versed philosopher. The objection, finally, that any philosophy whose ambition it is to bring into conformity its account of "reality" with the latest results of the sciences is doomed to "eternalize" highly transitory knowledge-claims, need likewise not endanger the position taken by Cassirer. It would be the alternative to the self-corrective character of the evidence trusted by him that would be fatal to any philosophy. The ambition to make final pronouncements, to issue "once-and-for-all" truths is certainly not germane to a thought-system which, by Kantian orientation, is not straining to lay hold upon a final reality-structure, but which is advanced frankly as an attempt to discharge the "culture-mission" of comprehending the various reality-accounts offered by the cultural disciplines and of indicating for them their specific type of symbolization.

We conclude therefore: the thesis that all contexts (in which we – objectively – have a world, structure, domain of reality) are to be interpreted as differently oriented symbolic evaluations of the data of perception, is offered (by Cassirer) as evidenced by all the inquiries made on these contexts. As such, the philosophy of symbolic forms is suggested as a generalization upon the pervasive features of the artistic, religious and scientific domains,

guided by Kant's transcendental axiom that the pervasive con-
nectious within all experience cannot be independent of the
synthesizing activities of a "symbol-minded" agent who generates
and reflects upon them.

We have given some indication of Cassirer's epistemological
commitment to Kant in the previous chapter, where we concluded
that Cassirer's position implied both an acceptance of Kant's
methodological strictures and a demand for a wider application
of his "critical method". More specifically: Kant's method was
to limit the theoretical philosophers' concern to an elucidation of
the modes of knowing which govern "reality" as scientifically
accessible. In consequence, it was to deny him the right of engaging in ontological pursuits for the purpose of discovering or
constructing "realities", offered as "metaphysical", whose apprehension would presuppose cognitive powers superior to those
certified as "constitutive" (or "regulative") for experience by
the first *Kritik*. Clearly, if science is recognized as the only legitimate medium through which the "objective" structure of experience can be known, philosophy, instead of competing with science,
may contribute by examining this (symbolic) medium, rather
than its experimentally controlled reference to experience.

If then the philosopher – as cognizor, not as moralizer – is to
be restricted to an analysis of the source, scope and validity of the
"mode of knowing" that makes possible experience as science;
or if, in Cassirer's extended version, he is to be restricted to an
examination of all the various modes of knowing and comprehending which make possible experience however structured (as
science or myth, art, religion or common-sense), the issue of highest philosophical universality will logically arise as that of attempting to reduce the variety of these distinguishable modes
of "having a world" to so many instances of one fundamental
(objectifying) function. Such a function would at once have to
be general enough to characterize all modes of knowing and
understanding, and it would yet have to permit of all the differentiations that specifically modify the various cultural media
for which it must account.

Now, it is Cassirer's contention that, historically, philosophy
both aimed at and fell short of, elaborating principles of such
generality as would, on the one hand, be valid for all domains

and, on the other, be susceptible of such modifications as could account for the specific differences distinguishing these domains. Before turning to a closer examination of the symbol-concept which, Cassirer thinks, satisfies the requirements for such a universal yet modifiable function, we must note here that Cassirer conceives of this objective as being in the general direction of what philosophers, with varying degrees of awareness and success, have always striven for.

In this connection, Cassirer has spoken of both the "culture-mission" of philosophy and of what he called the "antinomies of the culture-concept". Such "antinomies" are manifested by the conflicts which arise when the various cultural media of religion, art, language and science tend to set off their special domains by claiming superiority of insight for their respective perspectives. Thus, the first cosmologists, while they everywhere started out from the discriminations made by common sense and reflected by language, soon opposed to this basic fund of accumulated knowledge specifically new principles of discrimination and division, reaching for a "logos" from whose vantage-point all "non-scientific" knowledge appeared as a mere distortion of "the" truth. Similarly, although art and religion in their early stages developed closely together, if not at times in actual interpenetration, further development of these two cultural media resulted in one of them claiming superior vision of, and closer approximation to, the "really real" as over against the other. Instead of contenting themselves with the specific insights and reality-accounts which they indeed afford, the various cultural disciplines tend to impose the characteristic form of their interpretation upon the totality of being. It is from this tendency towards the "absolute" (or better: its partial interpretations), inherent in all of them, that there issue the conflicts which Cassirer terms "antinomial" within the culture-concept. In the face of intellectual conflicts of this type one would expect philosophy, as a reflection on the highest level of generality, to mediate between the various claims. However: "the dogmatic systems of metaphysics satisfy this expectation and demand only imperfectly; they themselves are immersed in this struggle and do not stand above it" [5]. It is suggested that, upon analysis, most philosophical systems turn out to be merely different hypostasized universalizations of a parti-

cular logical, ethical, esthetical or religious scheme of interpretation.

We have adduced these brief considerations because it is a-
gainst their background, I believe, that one can understand best
the importance Cassirer attributes to his own philosophy, which
is presented as having a chance of succeeding where all former
systems could only fail; not in the sense, to be sure, that it holds
the key to all the problems that have or will come up, but in the
sense, nevertheless, that with the symbol-concept there is put at
the philosopher's disposal an intellectual instrument of greatest
universality and modifiability. As such, it is commended as impartially comprehending every "domain of reality" as of a determinable, symbolically-mediate type, for which philosophical
analysis must indicate the specific modalities of sign-functioning
rather than super-impose one privileged modality of meaning,
with respect to which all other versions and visions become reduced to so many "approximations" and "appearances" at best,
or to "illusions" and "distortions" at worst.

In the light of the above, our earlier statement, namely that
Cassirer aimed to push beyond a "critique of reason" to a "critique
of culture", should be intelligible. As a matter of fact, however, his
theory of symbolic forms is presented in his *magnum opus* not so
much as a "critique", but rather as "prolegomena" for a future
philosophy of culture. The *Philosophie der Symbolischen Formen*,
if read from volume to volume, presents a sequence of analyses
of language, myth, religion, perceptual (commonsense), mathematical, and empirical knowledge. If read chapter by chapter in
each volume, it offers us analyses of such topics as space, time,
causality, number, objectivity, self, etc., which philosophers,
ancient and modern, have often claimed as properly belonging
to a metaphysics either of being or of experience. I can think of
no reason, therefore, why Cassirer's theory of symbolic forms
could not be expounded as both a "philosophy of culture" and
a "metaphysics of experience".

There is no doubt, of course, that Cassirer himself preferred to
think of his work as providing prolegomena for a philosophy of
culture. In this form his work was actually developed, starting
with a philosophy of language (Vol. I, 1923), moving on to a

philosophy of myth and religion (Vol. II, 1925) and to a philosophy of commensense and scientific knowledge (Vol. III, 1929). All that would seem to be required, however, to formulate Cassirer's analyses of language, myth and the sciences as a "metaphysics of experience" would be (1) to bring together the penetrating examinations of "mythical space", of the pragmatic "space of common sense", and of mathematical and physical "spaces"; (2) to arrange them within a single scheme of exposition; and (3) to do the same for the other "categories". The result would be at least as universal a treatment of the pervasive (symbolic) traits of being as is expected of a metaphysical treatise.

To develop Cassirer's work as a "metaphysics" may appear bold, if not outrightly paradoxical, in view of the frequent polemics against "metaphysical speculations" in his early writings and also in consideration of the pronounced anti-metaphysical tenor of the entire neo-Kantian movement, of which Cassirer was perhaps the most brilliant exponent. A somewhat closer examination of some of the relevant passages, however, will support our belief that this issue is essentially a terminological one. Cassirer's strictures concern not so much the possibility and legitimacy of metaphysics as a philosophical enterprise, as the questionability of what the word "metaphysics" has meant so far. Thus he says in *Substance and Function*: "When empirical science examines its own procedure, it has to recognize that there is in the (metaphysical) struggles a false and technical separation of ways of knowing that are both alike indispensable to its very existence. The motive peculiar to all metaphysics of knowing is here revealed. What appears and acts in the process of knowledge as an inseparable unity of conditions is hypostasized on the metaphysical view into a conflict of things" [6]. Now compare the above with another passage, written almost thirty years later: "The history of metaphysics is by no means a history of meaningless concepts or empty words ... it establishes a new basis of vision and from it gains a new perspective for knowing the real" [7]. What, on the surface, appears as a complete shift from a rejection to an acceptance of metaphysical thinking must be recognized, however, as a mere shift in emphasis with respect to an essentially identical point of view. To be sure, Cassirer's remarks in *Substance and Function* are not as positive with regard to metaphysics as when he asserts, in the *Hagerstrom* study, that "the genuine, the truly metaphysical thoughts have never been empty thoughts (or) thoughts without concepts" [8]. Still, it is in the context of the same study that he goes on to warn us, exactly as he did in his earlier work, that "... the difficulties, dangers and antinomies of metaphysics arise from the fact that its 'intuitions' themselves are not expressed in terms of their true methodological character. None (of the great metaphysical insights) is considered as giving insight into only a portion, but all are claimed as universally spanning the whole of reality ... The subsequent contest, resulting from such (partial) claims becomes at once a dialectical conflict" [9].

Cassirer's stand is consistent here. He does not side with the contention of the positivists that metaphysics is not only "false" but "meaningless". Instead, he is careful to distinguish the genuine character of the problems with which the great metaphysicians have dealt from the still imperfect manner in which their findings have come to us. The metaphysical results cannot be accepted without qualification, simply because metaphysicians have offered "partial truths" as "universal" ones. In focussing upon one or the other aspect of reality or perspective of symbolization (centering their systems around organic, artistic, logical, mathematical, mechanical, religious or ethical axioms), they have lost sight of the equal validity of such other aspects as must also be accounted for as legitimate paths to what, in every perspective, may be referred to as the "real".

Now, since this denial of a privileged status for any one form of symbolic representation of reality is exactly what Cassirer has claimed for his philosophy of symbolic forms, there does not seem to remain any reason why, according to his own pronouncements, his work may not indeed be considered as a type of metaphysics, oriented around the central notion of the symbol-concept. It is this concept which, for Cassirer, accounts for all aspects (contexts, "Sinnzusammenhänge") of the real, pervading as a common theme the polyphony of all cultural realms in which being is perceived, understood and known.

To summarize: if emphasis is put upon the most universal symbolic relations (space, time, cause, number, etc.) which appear in characteristic modifications in all cultural domains, we would be offered a metaphysics of (cultural) experience. If, on the other hand, our exposition proceeds by way of separate analyses of language, myth, religion, the mathematical and empirical sciences, then the character of Cassirer's work would more obviously be one of a philosophy of culture. Regardless, however, which form of presentation is chosen, each will center around the idea of the symbol-concept, of which a subsequent chapter will attempt a closer examination.

Cassirer himself, when offered an opportunity to make known his thought (in abbreviated form) to an English-speaking audience, sub-titled his *Essay on Man*: "An Introduction to a Philosophy of Human Culture". Here, the emphasis is on the cultural realities, the languages and rituals, the art-master-pieces and scientific procedures. To be comprehended philosophically they must be realized as so many symbolic manifestations of different types of synthesizing activities. "The content of the culture-concept cannot be separated from the basic forms and directions of significant (geistigen) production; their 'being' is understandable only as a 'doing'. It is only because there is a specific direction of our aesthetic imagination and intuition that we have a realm of aesthetic objects – and the same goes for all our other energies by virtue of which there is built up for us the structure of a specific domain of objectivity" [10].

True, an analysis of culture could proceed along different lines. To undertake a descriptive classification of the products of various cultural activities would appear to be just as legitimate as an attempt to seek "behind" this great diversity of manifestations for the characteristic types of intuiting, imagining and conceiving, the "doings" in the light of which the "works" become intelligible. As for the philosopher, however, he has no such choice. If he is to find a common denominator for all the worlds (realms of objectivity) in which he can move (emotionally, imaginatively, practically and theoretically), he must focus on the manifold forms of the "doings" even though, as a matter of fact, he cannot but infer them from the multiplicity of what is "done" by humans. In Cassirer's words: "We seek not a unity of effects but a unity of action; not a unity of products but a unity of the creative process" [11]. But this "unity of the creative process", as we shall see, can be nothing else but the unity and universality of that function which Cassirer ascribes to the symbol-concept.

In conclusion, it must be noted that on such a view the ,,culture-concept" must eclipse the "nature-concept" which, in Cassirer's earlier *Substance and Function* still figured as the concept of "lawfulness" (Gesetzmaessigkeit) as such. This becomes intelligible if one considers that whatever the "nature-concept" connotes at any given time is a function of what the cultural media of art, religion and science take it to mean.

"Whereas 'culture' creates, in an uninterrupted flow, ever new linguistic, artistic, religious and scientific symbols, both philosophy and science must break up these symbolic languages into their elements .... (We must learn) to interpret symbols in order to decipher the meaning-content they enclose, to make visible again the life from which they originally came forth" [12].

Measured against this gigantic task, what we have in the *Philosophie der Symbolischen Formen* must not be expected to provide a full and final answer. Surely, a more detailed and inclusive examination of the various cultural phenomena than can be offered by however great a single investigator would be required to make good the implied promise. Cassirer himself, aware of the preparatory character of his attempts in what he felt was the right direction, admits that his philosophy "cannot and does not try to be a philosophical system in the traditional sense of this word. All it attempted to furnish were the 'Prolegomena' to a future philosophy of culture ... Only from a continued collaboration between philosophy and the special disciplines of the 'Humanities' may one hope for a completion of this task" [13].

Recommendations for a collaboration between philosophy and the scientific (or other) disciplines have often been voiced by great philosophers. More recently, philosophers have been reproached for having neglected to keep in working touch with the mathematical and physical sciences. Cassirer's reminder to also stay in close touch with the humanities for a richer and more balanced accounting of the realities open to man, points to greater possibilities and responsibilities in the field of philosophy than are usually conceded by those who would restrict its relevance to a logical examination of the sciences of number and measurement. It will be the task of a final chapter to indicate some of the more important differences between a positivistically oriented "science of signs" (semiotic) and the objective of a "philosophy of symbolic forms". Before doing that, however, we must proceed to an exposition of the all-important symbol-concept, upon the proper understanding of which hinges Cassirer's conception both of what philosophy has been, and of what it must be if it is to give full and impartial attention to the phenomena of the "natural" as well as the "cultural" sciences.

CHAPTER III

THE SYMBOL CONCEPT I

EXPOSITION

The term "symbolic form" is employed by Cassirer in at least three distinct, though related, meanings:

(1) It covers what is often referred to as the "symbol concept', the "symbolic function" or simply the "symbolic" (das Symbolische).

(2) It denotes the variety of cultural forms which – as myth, religion, language and science – exemplify the realms of application for the symbol-concept.

(3) It is applied to space, time, cause, number, etc., all of which – as the most pervasive "symbolic relations" – are said to constitute such domains of "objectivity" as listed under (2).

In correspondence with these different usages, we shall first deal with (1) and attempt an adequate definition of the symbol-concept. We shall then examine the expressive, intuitional, and conceptual "modes" of the symbol-concept which are illustrated by what Cassirer calls the "symbolic forms" of myth (poetry), common-sense and science. (2) In a subsequent chapter, we shall see what happens to the space-concept, e.g., when it is taken as a "symbolic relation" (3) and followed through its mythical, common-sense and scientific modal forms (2) in the philosophy of symbolic forms. The purpose of our enterprise will be to show:

(a) that a consistent interpretation can be given of Cassirer's symbol-concept;

(b) that Cassirer's philosophy is best understood as a transition from a "critique of reason" to a "critique of culture" in that it suggests a widening of the scope of philosophic concern by putting the "transcendental question" beyond science to other types of institutionalized activities which, such as art, language, myth, religion, etc., actually define the meaning of "culture".

(c) that Cassirer's inquiry into symbolic forms may be read as a study of the basic (intuitional and categorical) relations (space, time, cause, number) and their characteristically different functioning in a greater variety of (cultural) contexts than are usually considered by the contemporary philosopher.

(I) EXPOSITION OF THE SYMBOL-CONCEPT

The symbol-concept, being the most universal concept within Cassirer's philosophy, is to cover the "totality of all phenomena which, in whatever form, exhibit 'sense in the senses' (Sinnerfüllung im Sinnlichen) and in which something 'sensuous' (ein Sinnliches) is represented as a particular embodiment of a 'sense' (meaning: Bedeutung) [1]. Here a definition of the symbol-concept is given by way of the two terms of the "sensuous" (broadly, the perceptually given) on the one hand and a "sense" (broadly, the meaning of any perceptually given) on the other, and a relation between the two which is most frequently referred to as "one representing the other". The extremely general character of this pronouncement must be noted. Cassirer's claim exceeds by far what has traditionally been admitted about "the symbolical character" of knowledge. While not all philosophers would subscribe to the idea that all knowledge is of a mediate type, it could safely be said that to the extent that it is taken to be a mediated rather than an immediate grasp of reality, it must also be taken as "symbolical" by virtue of its dependence upon (sets or systems of) symbols which determine the (discursive or mathematical) medium within which it is attained.

The history of ideas, disclosing a varying emphasis put by different thinkers upon sometimes one, sometimes another of the (symbolic) media to be trusted for the 'grand tour' to the 'really real', would indeed appear to exhibit confirming instances for Cassirer's trust in the universality of the symbolic function. All human "sense-making", whether cognitive or not, is defined by him as implying (besides an interpretant, mind, *Geist*, etc.), both: a) the givenness of perceptual signs (sensuous vehicles, *ein Sinnliches*) and b) something signified (meaning, *Sinn*). This definition would surely be wide enough to cover a considerable area of agreement between otherwise quite distinct philosophies with respect to their common recognition of the symbolically-mediate character of knowledge; but note that it formulates no restrictions to cognitive discourse. The "representative" relation which is asserted to hold between the "senses" and their (signified) "sense" is not taken to be exhaustively definable by grammatical, logical and mathematical syntax-types, nor even by the semantical rules which determine the conventional languages of common-sense and science. Instead, the symbolic function covers "the whole range of phenomena within which there is 'sense in the senses', i.e., all contexts in which experience is either reflected upon or simply where it is 'had' as of "characters and persons" (on the "expressive" level of symbol-functioning) or of "things" in space and time (on the intuitional level of symbol-functioning).

How about the issue of confronting "facts" and "symbols" for the purpose of confirmation, germane to all views which consider the cognitive dimension of symbol-situations exclusively? Can it even come up for a philosophy according to which "facts" cannot be evidence for (or against) "symbols", if only because their very "factuality" is not considered meaningful outside of some determinate symbolic context? The objection, often raised against scholasticism, namely that it replaced the consideration of facts (nature) by a manipulation of symbols (names) need, however, not invalidate Cassirer's position for which "there is no factuality... as an absolute... immutable datum; but what we call a fact is always theoretically oriented in some way, seen in regard to some... context and implicitly determined thereby. Theoretical elements do not somehow become added to a 'merely factual', but they enter into the definition of the factual itself" [2]. Once the "facts" or "state of affairs", designated by symbols, are interpreted as themselves exhibiting context (i.e. expressive or perceptual modes of representation), the question of the "control" of symbols by facts would have to be replaced by the question concerning the "checking" of one (discursive) symbol-context by another (perceptual) one, considered more reliable or more easily instituted by the human observer.

In this connection, a brief glance at the issue of confirmation may be to the point. In Carnap's version: "the scientist describes his own observations concerning a certain planet in a report O_1.

Further, he takes into consideration a theory T, concerning the movements of planets (also such other theories as would justify the application of his instruments. CH). From O_1 and T the astronomer deduces a prediction; he calculates the apparent position of the planet for the next night. At that time, he will make a new observation and formulate it in a report O_2. Then he will compare the prediction P with O_2 and thereby find it either confirmed or not" [3].

A theoretical symbolism, in other words, is confirmed when the phenomena, predicted by the symbolism, are observed. Admittedly, however, there is a hypothetical reference to context not only in the theory to be confirmed but also in the observations which do the confirming. "All observation"- writes Lenzen – "involves more or less explicitly the element of hypothesis" [4]. Thus, to say that a theory (in combination with statements regarding initial conditions) is confirmed by observation would not at all require recognition of, and recourse to, any "non-symbolic" facts, disclosed to the senses free from all elements of hypothesis and interpretation. On the view proposed by Cassirer, it would be preferable to say that hypothetically constructed contexts (theories regarding the orbit of a planet) would be confirmable if certain data can be deduced from it, (e.g., its position at a given time) such that, by a rule-determined coordination of a perceptual context, what are defined as "masses" and "light-emissions" in one context will be interpreted as the determinate color and shape of a "thing" (planet) in another.

Furthermore: we have an "interpretant" with his attendant "perspectives", a "sign-signified"-relation on the theoretical as well as on the observational levels. To hold that the former stands in need of confirmation by the latter, to maintain that "the scientific criterion of objectivity rests upon the possibility of occurrence of predicted perceptions to a society of observers" [5], is fully intelligible within the provisions of Cassirer's view which cannot except observation from a "symbolic" interpretation. Whether as observation of pointer-readings or of things, the confirmatory character of observation does not depend upon confronting symbolic theories with "non-symbolic" facts but rather upon the readily controlled and publicly shareable nature of the perceptual context in which we have "facts" and to which

all other contexts can be co-ordinated in varying degrees of ex-
plicitness. We suggest, therefore, that whereas the import of
symbolic media for the intelligibility of reality is certainly not a
new discovery and has been realized by philosophers from Plato
to Dewey, the thesis that a symbolic relation obtains for every
possible (even any per-ceptual) context in which we "have" a
world, expresses what is most distinctive in Cassirer's philosophy of symbolic forms.

We must now examine more closely what exactly is asserted
when it is said of the "constitutive" and "cultural" forms which
condition reality that they are "symbolical". For this purpose,
let us go back to the definition of the symbol-concept according
to which "it is to cover the totality of all those phenomena which
exhibit in whatever form 'sense in the senses' (Sinnerfüllung im
Sinnlichen) and all contexts in which a sense-datum, by being
what it is (in der Art seines Da-Seins und So-Seins), is represented
as a particular embodiment, as a manifestation and incarnation
of a meaning" [6]. According to this passage, the symbol-concept
would apply to all contexts in which a sense-datum may be
distinguished from the sense or meaning it carries, with the
proviso that a relation holds with respect to these two terms
which is most frequently referred to as "one representing the
other". For Cassirer (as for most other philosophers) "sense-
datum" (ein Sinnliches) covers all those cues which, as colors,
sounds, etc., can act as vehicles for any and all meanings, where
"meaning" covers all the "embodiments" to which sense-data
are amenable when related to an "interpreter" of these cues, i.e.,
to the full complexity of perspectives which the term "interpreter" (mind, Geist, Bewusstsein) suggests.

To realize yet more distinctly what both the "sensory"- and the
"sense"- moments connote in this definition, we must attempt a
closer examination of the relation that is supposed to hold between the two terms if they are to function symbolically. This
relation, it will be seen, is presented by Cassirer as both polar and
correlative in nature.

(*1*) *The Polarity of "sense" and "senses"*

Stressing the polarity of this relation, Cassirer states succinctly that "the symbolic function is composed of moments which are different in principle. No genuine meaning as such is simple, but it is a "one and other" (eins und doppelt) and this polarity which is intrinsic to it, does not tear it asunder or destroy it, but instead represents its proper function" [7]. This function, then, establishes a relation between the senses, as signs, and their sense, as signified by them, in such a way that these two terms must be conceived as polar, opposite and (potentially, if not actually) distinguishable from each other. This distinction of the two symbol-moments, as maintained by Cassirer, can be read from a variety of pronouncements made apropos the three modal forms, termed respectively:

(a) the expression-function (Ausdrucksfunktion)
(b) the intuitional function (Anschauungsfunktion)
(c) the conceptual function (reine Bedeutungsfunktion).

We must now proceed to consider separately how the "polar relation" between sign and signified, senses and sense, data and meaning is conceived by Cassirer in these three basic modal functions.

(a) If the relation between sense-data and their sense is of an expressive type (encountered in myth, art and the realization of persons), "reality" is had as a universe of "characters", with all events in it having physiognomic traits and all manifestation of "sense" through the "senses" being restricted to what becomes experienceable within man's "emotive-affective" perspective. On this level, both moments can only "potentially" be separated. Actually, it is the very character of expression-phenomena that they present "sign and signified" in a fusion which knows of no difference between the "picture" and the "pictured", between the sense-vehicle and the sense it carries. This peculiar type and direction of signification is misrepresented by the usual "symbolic" interpretations of myth, be they theoretical or moral, according to which a "sensus mythicus" is to be distinguished from a "sensus allegoricus" and a "sensus anagogicus", or for which myth figures merely as an allegorical-symbolic language which both conceals and reveals secret and profound meanings. Instead, "it is exactly this separation of the ideal from the real, this hiatus between a world of immediate being and a world of mediate meanings, this opposition between picture and thing, which is foreign to mythical thought" [8]. It is us, the observers, who, not living in myth anymore, project this opposition into it. As Cassirer concludes from an examination of a great many forms of name- and picture-magic (which have challenged anthropologists ever since they were noted); "The word (picture) does not stand for the thing (person, God), it is it" [9].

Where the world is still taken in its primary expression-values, all of its phenomena manifest a specific character which belongs to them in an immediate and spontaneous fashion. Cassirer's description of these phenomena as being inherently sombre or cheerful, exciting or appeasing, reassuring or frightening" [10] parallels Dewey's account, according to which "empirically. things are poignant, tragic, settled, disturbed ... are such immediately and in their own right and behalf ... Any quality as such is final; it is at once initial and terminal; just what it is as it exists" [11].

It would therefore be a misreading of the "expression-phenomena" if they were taken to issue from secondary acts of interpretation or as products of "acts of empathy". The basic error of such "explanations" would be that they reverse the order of what is phenomenally given; they "must destroy the character of perception, reduce it to a mere complex of sensory data of impression, in order to then revive the dead matter of perception by an act of empathy" [12]. What is overlooked in all such "Einfühlungs"-theories is that in order to get at the sensory data (the hot and the cold, the hard and the soft, the colors, sounds, etc.), one must already have abstracted them from the primary expression-phenomena in which a "world" is had prior to the working out of the various representational and conceptual schemes through which man, by taking less "emotive" and more "practical" and "theoretical" perspectives, eventually learns to "explain" and orientate himself in more sober and less dramatic sign-interpretations. Briefly then: what typifies an expression-phenomenon is not that, on the level of reflection, a distinction between the sensory data and their meaning cannot be made, but rather that, on the level of its own realization, no such distinction between the two polar moments of symbolic functioning is as yet possible. A fuller discussion of the expression-mode of the symbol-concept will be attempted in a later chapter.

(b) The polarity between the "sensory"- and the "sense"-moments is encountered in more developed form in what Cassirer calls the intuitional (Anschauungs-)mode of the symbol-concept. Here a perception is not merely taken as a qualitative presentation (Präsenz) but as a cue for the representation of something else. "The construction of our perceptual world begins with such acts of dividing up the ever-flowing series of sense-phenomena. In the midst of this steady flux of phenomena there are now retained certain determinate units which, from now on, serve as fixed centers of orientation. The particular phenomenon could not have any characteristic meaning except as referred to those centers. And all further progress of objective knowledge, all clarification and determination of our perceptual world depend on this ever-progressing development" [13]. Here the passage from the expression- to the intuitional mode of making "sense through the senses" is described by Cassirer as a development in which an "organization" of the "sensory flux" is brought about in such a way that its "data", instead of merely signifying their own immediate and emotive meaning, can refer to and represent each other; this, of course, involves a singling out of certain data, realized as comparatively relevant for action, a division of the sense-data into "presentative" and "representative" ones. Now: the selective and organizing nature of sensory perception has long been noted by both scientists and philosophers. To put a "symbolic" interpretation upon whatever evidence exists for this notion, is done because "selectivity" does presuppose a distinction between the "constant" and the "variable", the "necessary" and the "contingent", the "general" and the "particular", a distinction which, in turn, presupposes "points of view", teleologically determined "foci of attention", from which sense-data become differently evaluated for their representative possibilities. On this interpretation, an "object", instead of being apprehended *ab extra* or as a terminus for a causal inference from perceptions (Russell), is interpreted as a "representative relationship" obtaining among the perceptions themselves, in such a manner, furthermore, that these perceptual data are divided into relatively constant and relatively fleeting ones, with the latter representing the more constant ones to which they "adhere" as to their centers, as "properties" adhering to (or representing) "things".

The "thing-property"-relationship, accordingly, appears on what Cassirer calls the intuitional (or Anschauungs-)level of symbolic reference. For evidence, supporting this interpretation, Cassirer points to the "constancy-phenomena", described by Hering and the investigations on plane and surface colors, carried on by such physiologists and psychologists as Helmholtz, Katz and Buehler, upon which he generalizes as follows: sense-data (optical phenomena, e.g.), unless felt in their immediate expression-value, are experienced representatively when a variety of strictly different colors are taken as signs of one constant color attributed to a "thing". On the other hand, one and the same color (e.g., a bright mark on a dark path) could represent quite *different* things: a spot of light, if its brightness is causally connected with a sunbeam, or simply a bit of white chalk, sprinkled on the path, if a thing-property relation is assumed between the color seen and the "thing" of which it is the color. In Cassirer's words: "The organization of our perceptual world is symbolical to the extent that some sensory impressions, as comparatively variable ones, are made signs of comparatively more constant ones which they signify" [14]. Among contemporary American philosophers, C. I. Lewis arrives at an almost identical interpretation. "That feature of perceptual cognition which consists in the attachment to the given content of a meaning or a significance of something other than this content of awareness itself, is often called its character as 'mediate' or its function as 're-presenting'. And what is thus 'mediated' or 'represented' is the 'object of knowledge' – in our example, the thing perceived out there in space" [15].

Cassirer refers to language as both the outstanding agency which establishes basic objectifying distinctions among our sensory data, and as the medium which reflects the "foci of attention", the "perspectives" which determine whatever discrimination is exercised when some, rather than other, perceptual data are taken to "represent" the quasi-permanent units in which, on the intuitional mode of symbolization, we have a "world" as organized in spatio-temporal "things-with-properties". Reserving for a more appropriate context an examination of the evidence adduced by Cassirer for this "objectifying" office of language, what matters for the present purpose is that the intuitional mode of symbolic representation is again conceived as involving, besides the sensory-moment, a distinguishable "meaning", and "original mode of sight" (eine eigene Weise der Sicht). Both of these moments are said to stand in a polar relationship to each other insofar as the "sight", the "perspectives', which organize the sensory flux, are not reducible to, or constructible from, the sensory data, which are "seen" and interpreted from their various angles as thing-properties.

Cassirer argues in this connection against both rationalistic and empiricist epistemologies which, regardless of how differently they provide answers to the question of the "relation of perceptions to an object", take the same basic course in explaining this relation either in terms of "associations" and "reproductions" or in terms of "unconscious inferences". "What is overlooked in either approach is the circumstance that all psychological or logical processes to which one has recourse come rather too late.. No associative connection of them can explain that original 'mode of positing' (Setzungsmodus) through which an impression, taken representatively, stands for something 'objective'." [16]. The intuitional (Anschauungs-)mode is proposed therefore as both an original and ultimate form of "sight" which, although actually not separable from the sensory data "seen", is to be distinguished from them as sharply as the dimension of "meaning" (sense) from the dimension of "signs" (senses).

(c) The polar relation between the "sensory-" and "sense-" moments is more clearly realized in Cassirer's discussion of the conceptual mode of the symbol-function. In this dimension, also referred to as the "level of cognition", there is, as within the expression and intuitional modes, an organization of the sensory data; there is this difference, however, that now "the moments which condition the order and structure of the perceptual world are grasped as such and recognized in their specific significance. The relations which (before) were established "implicitly" (in der Form blosser Mitgegebenheit) are now explicated" [17]. Thus, things have been enumerated, magnitudes compared, equivalences of groups have been established long before the procedures, consistent with the arithmetical number-concept, were abstractly isolated and realized in their "pure" (analytical) validity. This tendency towards the isolation of relations which,

though applicable to perception, are in principle of a non-per-
ceptual and non-expressive nature, is evidenced and "writ large"
in the constructive schemata, the conventional systems of order-
signs which symbolically mediate scientific knowledge.

There is, for Cassirer, no real break of continuity between
these constructive symbolisms of science and the language-signs
of common sense. "What is done unconsciously in language, is
consciously intended and methodically performed in the scientific
process. But while this process of determination by means of
conventional signs begins with language, it assumes an entirely
new shape in science. For the symbolism of number is quite a
different logical type from the symbolism of speech. In language,
we find the first efforts of classification, but these are still un-
coordinated ... Every single linguistic term has a special area
of meaning. It is (as Gardiner says) 'a beam of light, illuminating
first this portion, then that portion of the field within which the
thing, or rather the complex concatenation of things, signified
by a sentence, lies'. But all these different 'beams of light' do not
have a common focus. They are dispersed and isolated ... This
state of affairs is completely changed as soon as we enter into the
realm of number. We cannot speak of isolated numbers. A single
number is only a single place in a general systematic order ...
Numbers originate in one and the same generative relation, that
relation which connects a number 'n' with its immediate successor
(n plus 1) ... In the theories of Frege, Russell, of Peano and
Dedekind, number has lost all its ontological secrets and the
introduction of new classes of numbers does not create new objects but new symbols. The new numbers (fractional or irrational)
are symbols not of simple relations but of relations of relations ..
in order to fill the gap between the integers (which are discrete
qualities) and the world of physical events, contained in the con-
tinuum of space and time, mathematical thought was bound to
find a new instrument. If number had been a 'thing', a 'substantia
quae in se est et per se concipitur', the problem would have been
insoluble. But since it was a symbolic language, it was only
necessary to develop the vocabulary, the morphology and the
syntax of this language in a consistent way" [18].

The thesis that all theoretical thought is constructive of relational schemata (analogous to the type outlined above with

respect to number or to Descartes' transformation of geometrical problems in his analytical geometry) was developed by Cassirer in considerable detail in his *Substance and Function* (Berlin, 1910), where all scientific concept-formation is defined as an ever-widening and increasingly precise application of "relational thinking". In the concluding sections of the *Philosophie der Symbolischen Formen*, recent developments of the mathematical and physical sciences are once more considered as confirming evidence for his early theory of concept-formation.

What about this theory? According to Cassirer, what the concept establishes is variously referred to as a "function", a "principle", a "law of a series", a "rule" or "form", where all these terms are employed with the same connotation that had been given in his early *Substance and Function*, i.e., as expressing relations between (terms designating) phenomena. Or, as he put it later, to comprehend conceptually and to establish relations turn out, upon a thorough logical and epistemological analysis, to be always correlative notions" [19]. Accordingly, Cassirer takes exception to the manner in which classical logic defines the concept as the "class-unit" under which individuals (or species) are subsumed. Instead, the concept establishes a "unity of relation" by virtue of which a manifold is determined as belonging together within the series (law) which is specified by this relation. Rather than defining concepts as extensively determining a class having members, it should be realized that theoretical concepts "always contain reference to an exact serial principle that enables us to connect the manifold of intuition in a definite way, and to run through it according to a prescribed law ... (Thus) no insuperable gap can occur between the 'universal' and the 'particular', because the universal itself has no other meaning and purpose than to represent and to render possible the connection and order of the particulars. If we regard the particular as a serial member and the universal as a serial principle, it is at once clear that the two moments, without going over into each other and in any way being confused, still refer throughout in their function to each other" [20].

For an examination of the adequacy of this "concept-theory" to specific scientific issues, the reader is referred to the relevant sections in *Substance and Function, Determinismus und Indetermi-*

nismus in der modernen Physik (1940) and Cassirer's studies on
Einstein's Theory of Relativity. To consider briefly just one illustration: the "energy-concept" derives its scientific meaning from
a number of relational steps. We begin with the establishment of
certain empirically observable dependency-series; the manifold
actual observations, arranged in each series and at first appearing
to be isolated and independent of each other, are eventually
connected by a relation of equivalence such that there corresponds
to a value in one series one and only one value of the other. By
taking more and more types of physical processes into account,
we extend this equivalence-connection until finally, grounded by
observations and deductions, we draw the conclusion that with
respect to every type of physical phenomena, we shall find that
definite relations of equivalence will hold for them. The strict,
scientific meaning of the "energy-concept" is thus exhausted in
the application of a transitive and symmetrical relation for every
type of physical process, so that a definite "quantity of energy"
can be coordinated to every member of a compared series.

The above allusions, while surely not sufficient to argue Cassirer's theory of concept-formation, may suffice, at least, to support his contention that on the conceptual mode of symbol-
functioning we must again realize a clear-cut distinction between
the "sense" or "principle" of a series and the "sensory" manifold
ordered by it as "members of the series". For purposes of further
highlighting this polarity between the two moments of the
symbol-concept, Cassirer frequently employs the language of
symbolic logic. If, instead of defining a concept extensionally,
we do so in terms of a propositional function $p(x)$, we are clearly
designating two distinct moments. "The general form of the
function designated by the letter 'p' is to be sharply contrasted
with the values of the variable 'x' which may enter this function
as true values. The function determines the relation of these
values, but it is not itself one of them: the 'p' of 'p(x)' is not
homogenous to the 'x_1, x_2, x_3 ... x_n'" [21]. Both, the 'p' and the
'x', in other words, designate different moments of conceptual-
ization.

What Cassirer maintains is not so much – as has been assumed –
that the "serial concept" must be opposed to the "class-concept",

but rather that the latter is more consistently interpreted as a special type of the former. In his contention that concepts, "concrete" or "abstract", "universal", "general" or "singular", are concisely symbolized by the formula 'p(x)', Cassirer would seem to share one view of Russell which the latter has held through the years, namely that a concept, as a term, standing for a class, must be considered an incomplete symbol which, to be completed, requires propositional integration [22].

For symbolic language, no definition of a concept could take a smaller unit than the "p(x)"-form for any "S-P"-type proposition, or the "p(x,y..n)" form for richer relational combinations. To illustrate: the term "chair" designates a concept only on condition that the property of "being a chair" can be made definite enough to determine a realm of application; only then will we know what to look for, or ground such assertions as "x is a chair", "y is a chair", etc. In this form, the term "chair", as a property, defines (limits the scope of) a class of chairs only in so far as it is recognized to have features which, as instances of that property, make it a member of a class defined by that property. Thus: terms stand for concepts only if they are, or can be, formulated propositionally. If so formulated, they throw into relief the distinctness of the two moments of symbolic representation: the sense, principle or form of a series and its "sensory"-, observational- or "material'" members. What is distinctive of scientific concept-formation, on the other hand, is not the manifold of sensation to which its serial relations apply but the elaboration of distinctive "points of view" which, as principles, theories or laws, determine the perspective, selection and organization of the perceptually given into specifically ordered series. It is for this reason that Cassirer objects, on many occasions, to those empiricist doctrines which regard the "similarity" of perceived objects or properties as a self-evident psychological fact, and hence as fit to account for the serial relations established by scientific concepts. In his *Substance and Function* he declares that "the similarity of certain elements can only be spoken of significantly when a certain point of view has been established from which the elements can be designated as like or unlike. The difference between these contents, on one hand, and the conceptual species by which we unify them, on the other, is an irreducible fact; it is categorical.." [23]. It designates, we could say now, the polar contrast between the member of the series and the form of the series.

With the above in mind, it will be intelligible why Cassirer holds that the relationship of "representation" which is said to obtain between the two moments that make up the definition of the symbol-concept in its expressive, intuitional and conceptual modes, must be thought of as a "polarity", with the sensory data on one hand, and a sense or meaning on the other.

(2) *The Correlativity of "sense" and the "senses"*

We have now considered a number of passages indicative of Cassirer's conviction that for all levels on which we symbolically "have" a world (be it as organized in qualitative expression characters, be it as broken into spatio-temporally ordered "things-with-properties" or in the relational order-systems of the sciences), we are always in a position to make a 'distinctio rationis' between the "sight" (or "form" of a manifold) and the "sense-data" that represent different meanings within different "sights". We have pointed out that this conviction implied an interpretation of "polarity" with respect to two defining moments of the symbol-concept. In the sequence, we must qualify this characterization and give attention to such other passages in his work as would tie the two symbol-moments together so closely that, in spite of their "polar distinguishability", neither of them appears definable except under the implicit presupposition of the meaning of the other. If, in consonance with Cassirer's actual usage, we call the sensory manifold the "matter" and the sense-perspective (Sinn-Perspektive) the "form" of the symbol-concept, then we are bidden to think of these terms in a correlativity such that it is not only impossible to separate one from the other in any actual context, but also in such a way that no meaning can be assigned to either (formal or material) term without implicit reference to the other. At this point, it appears, our problem makes contact with the traditional controversy about universals. From what has been said already, there can be no doubt that Cassirer will not side, without qualifications, with either the "realist" or the "nominalist" positions. The "realists", in his view, were

mistaken in establishing a hiatus so strict between the "universal
form" and the "particular matter" that the embodiment of one
in the other remained unintelligible. His charge against nominal-
ists is that they attempted to "grab the universal (concept) with
their bare hands" [24]. St. Thomas' dictum "universalia non sunt
res subsistentes, sed habent esse solum in singularibus" is quoted
by him approvingly as expressing a "strict correlation, a mutual
relationship between the general and the particular" [25]. What
attracts Cassirer to this version is the circumstance that it is free
of the various space-and time-metaphorical attributes that are
usually used in the characterization of the "universal" as being
"before" or "after", "within" or "outside" the particular. Instead, Cassirer emphasizes throughout that "form" and "matter"
can be defined only "correlatively", that the "sight" determines
the very quality of the "seen", that the "principle" of a series
exhausts its meaning in the order it establishes among its members, that the "p" of a propositional function cannot be defined
in independence from its value-range. Russell has put this last
point lucidly: "It is to be observed that, according to the theory
of propositional functions, the O in O_x is not a separate and distinguishable entity; it lives in the proposition of the form O_x and
cannot survive analysis ... If O were a distinguishable entity,
there would be a proposition asserting O of itself, which we may
denote by $O(O)$; there would also be a proposition "not $O(O)$",
denying $O(O)$. In this proposition, we may regard O as variable;
we thus obtain a propositional function. The question arises:
can the assertion in this propositional function be asserted of
itself? The assertion is non-assertible of itself, hence it can be
asserted of itself; it cannot, and if it cannot, it can. This contradiction is avoided by the recognition that the functional part
of a propositional function is not an independent entity" [26].

In Cassirer's language: the "perspective" of an ordered whole
cannot be conceived in independence of the perceptual elements
which it orders; we have no way of getting at the meaning of the
sensory (or material-) moment of the symbol concept since it can
neither be encountered nor conceived as stripped from all and
any relationship to some "sense", "form" or "perspective".

For a closer examination of the "correlative" characterization
of the relationship of representation between the two moments

defining the symbol concept and the extent to which it is compatible with the "polarity" so frequently stressed by Cassirer, we will now turn to a consideration of and, if possible, a defense against, objections which have been raised against the inner consistency of the symbol-concept.

CHAPTER IV

THE SYMBOL CONCEPT II

OBJECTIONS AND DEFENSE

In our exposition of the symbol-concept, we have so far come
to two results: *a*) The two moments which, as the "sense" and
"senses", stand in a relationship of representation with respect
to each other, are distinguishable, polar and, at least on the level
of reflection, "independently variable". *b*) It is asserted that
neither moment is actually encounterable nor even conceivable
except correlatively to the other. Are these two results compatible
with each other? The Swedish philosopher Konrad Marc-Wogau [1] has maintained that they are not. He has accordingly
suggested that the symbol-concept, as conceived by Cassirer, is
not free from contradictions on the grounds that the two moments
by which he aims to define it cannot both: 1) belong to two
entirely different dimensions, and 2) yet belong together so
closely that the definition of one could not be given except in
terms of the other. It is to these objections that we must now
give some attention.

Marc-Wogau writes: "A closer examination seems to me to
lead to the result that the positive meaning of Cassirer's "symbolic relation" is of a dialectical character; the symbolic relation, as conceived by Cassirer, covers both the idea of an opposition between the sensuously given (the sign) on the one hand,
and the "Sinnerfüllung" (the signified) on the other, and also
the idea of an identity between the two. The first idea is clearly
asserted by Cassirer, the second issues as a consequence from
certain of his definitions and assertions" [2]. Now, the second idea
concerns the correlativity of the two symbol-moments which,
according to Marc-Wogau, entails their identity as a consequence.
Let us follow his reasoning: " 'Sign' and 'Signified' . . . are to be
mutually conditioned by each other in their determinate character. One moment has meaning only in relation to the other. But
that implies that the thought about the one term involves the

thought about the other. If the one term is being thought of, the other is thereby being thought of, too. The two moments of the relation would, in consequence, coincide. If A and B are to be connected in such a way that A can be determined only with reference to B and if B can be determined only in reference to A, it becomes impossible to distinguish A and B: they coincide" [3].

With respect to another characterization of the symbol-concept, according to which it is said to be "immanence" and "transcend-ance" in one [4] (expressing, as it does, a non-sensory meaning in sensory data) Marc-Wogau remarks: "In this definition, two moments are distinguished which are related in a specific way. When Cassirer characterizes this relation by saying that "the symbol is not 'the one or the other' but that it represents the 'one in the other' and the 'other in the one' ", the question seems to crop up how, under such circumstances, a possible distinction between the 'one' and the 'other' could even be made. By this definition, is there not posited an identity between the two moments of the symbolic relation which would conflict with the insistence upon their polarity?" [5].

In Cassirer's rejoinder to these objections [6] at least two differ-ent lines of argumentation can be distinguished. One argument questions Marc-Wogau's conviction that there are logical grounds on which the maintained correlativity of the two symbol-moments could be refuted. Furthermore, illustrations drawn from empirical sciences are reproduced for the purpose of supporting Cassirer's contention that these two moments (although correlative) cannot only still be distinguished, but also showing that and how such isolation of the two moments has been accomplished. In this connection, Cassirer quotes extensively from contemporary re-search into color- and acoustical phenomena which are presented by him as documenting in *fact* what Marc-Wogau had denied as a *possibility*.

(1) The Logical Issue

Marc-Wogau's objection that, if two terms of a relation are thought of as "mutually determined", they will, of necessity, also be "identical", is countered by Cassirer's reference to the actual employment of "implicit definitions" in modern mathematics. Now, implicit definitions have been defined as "denoting anything whatsoever provided that what they denote conforms to stated relations between themselves" [7], where the stating of the relations is conceded to be given within a selected axiom-set. With the discovery of non-Euclidean geometries, Cassirer remarks, it became increasingly clear to those concerned with their logical foundation that their elements – the points, lines, angles, etc. – could not anymore be defined in the explicit fashion of Euclid, who took them as intuitively evident. "Neither the basic elements, nor the basic relations (of non-Euclidean geometries) could have been defined, if by a definition one understands the indication of the 'genus proximum' and of the 'differentia specifica' " [8]. A way out of this difficulty, Cassirer suggests [9], was opened by Pasch's investigations, which were continued and brought to a systematic conclusion with Hilbert's *Grundlagen der Geometrie*. Hilbert's analyses may be summarized by saying that, for him, the geometrical elements and relations are not to be taken as independent entities, grasped intuitively, for which explicit definitions can be given, but rather as terms whose meaning is specified by the relations which are axiomatically prescribed for them. "The axioms which they satisfy determine and exhaust their essence" [10]. Basic geometrical concepts are, accordingly, held to be definable only implicitly, i.e., within a logical system; and it is gratuitous to ask for a determination of their meaning independently of such a system. It follows that, if in Hilbert's view the signification of points, lines, the relations of "between-ness", "outside", etc., cannot be formulated except in relation to a selected axiom-group, then a variety of other elements and relations – if they satisfy these same formal conditions – would have to be considered as equivalent to them. Against the very possibility of such structural isomorphisms, of different (though logically justifiable) interpretations of the same basic calculus, the objection has been raised that this merely proves the impossibility of arriving at completely determined elements by means of implicit definitions. This apparent limitation, however, also marks the very strength of mathematical, deductive thought. As Cassirer puts it in *Substance and Function*: "Two different types of assertions, of which one deals with straight lines and planes, the other with cycles and spheres ...

are regarded as equivalent to each other insofar as they provide
for the same conceptual dependencies ... The points with which
Euclidean geometry deals can be changed into spheres and circles,
into inverse point-pairs of a hyperbolic or elliptical group of
spheres ... without any change being produced in the deductive
relations of the individual propositions ... evolved for these
points ... Mathematics recognizes (in these points) no other
'being' than that belonging to them by participation in this form.
For it is only this 'being' that enters into proof and into the processes of inference and is thus accessible to the full certainty that
mathematics gives to its subject-matter" [11].

The relevance of these considerations for the problem at hand
could be put thus: Marc-Wogau's proposal that, if the terms of a
relation are mutually determined, they thereby must also be
identical, can be dismissed if we maintain the justifiability of
implicit definitions and the different calculi which they entail.
And vice-versa: Marc-Wogau's charge, if taken seriously, would
invalidate not only the "logic of the symbol-concept" but also
the "logic" of all those logical and mathematical disciplines which
require implicit definitions for the constitution of their different
syntax-types. Cassirer suggests therefore that, if the scientist
can proceed effectively with elements whose meaning is definable
only within the axiom-system where they occur, the philosopher
neither may nor need hope for a more secure foundation regarding
the symbol-concept. The charge of contradiction inherent in this
concept is countered by Cassirer's reference to scientific syntax
whose elements are not considered "identical" merely because
their definition involves "correlative" determination.

(2) *The Empirical Issue*

Regardless, however, of whether the "correlativity" of the two
symbol-moments implies their "identity" or not, are there any
other than the above "formal" considerations supporting Cassirer's thesis that a distinction between these moments is not
only logically permissible but also actually achievable? Before
looking at the evidence to which Cassirer refers in answer to this
question, it may be worthwhile to consider the issue here raised
in its full generality.

We have, in an earlier chapter, indicated how the development of the symbol-concept was related to Kant's epistemology, insofar as it was to cover all the "synthesizing acts" which variously determine the expressive-, intuitional- and conceptual-structures in which we have the respective worlds of myth, art, common sense and science. Instead of departing from a taken-for-granted opposition between a statically conceived "self" (mind, Geist, reason, etc.) and an equally static "world" (reality, experience, objects), the philosophy of symbolic forms is proposed as an examination of "the presuppositions upon which that opposition depends and to state the conditions that are to be satisfied if it is to come about. It finds that these conditions are not uniform, that there are rather different dimensions of apprehending, comprehending and knowing the phenomena and that, relative to this difference, the relationship between 'self' and 'world' is capable of characteristically different interpretations ... True, all these forms aim at objectification on the level of perception (zielen auf gegenständliche Anschauung hin); but the perceived objects change with the type and direction of such objectification. The philosophy of symbolic forms, accordingly, does not intend to establish a special dogmatic theory regarding the essence and properties of these 'objects', but it aims, instead, at a comprehension of these types of objectification which characterize the arts as well as religion and science" [12].

It follows that, if there is no structure (of 'being' or 'experience') except within the symbolic forms of myth, religion, art, common sense and the sciences, then there can also be no chance ever to break out of the "charmed circle" of these forms. If, therefore, it is only under the presupposition of the pervasiveness of these forms that we can "apprehend, comprehend and know" objects, however structured, how will it indeed be possible even to conceive of the "sensory" (material) moment of the symbol-function as "polar" and distinct from the "sense" (or formal) moment? What answer, in other words, can be given to Marc-Wogau's charge that, to be consistent, Cassirer cannot hope to make even a "distinctio rationis" between the perceptual, sensory-, and the perspectival, sense-aspects, both of which are required for that relation of "representation" which defines the meaning of the symbol-concept? It is typical of Cassirer's procedure that the

resolution of this question is not left to purely logical or specifically "philosophical" arguments of the kind which are conventionally devoted to the "form-matter"-issue. Instead, Cassirer prefers
to evaluate the issue in the light of available empirical evidence.
Let us be clear about exactly which issue the empirical reference
is to provide evidence. What is under discussion concerns the
question whether the "material" moment of the symbol-concept
(to which we have variously referred as "sense-data", the "perceptual" or "sensory" manifold, etc.) can, if not actually encountered, then at least be conceived as distinct from the "formal" moment (to which we have variously referred as the "sense",
"meaning", "perspective", "principle", "sight", etc.). For evidence of the fact that this problem has been recognized by scientists, Cassirer quotes these remarks from the German psycholo-
gist Karl Buehler: "No theory of perception should forget that
already the most simple qualities, such as 'red' and 'warm'
usually do not function for themselves but as signs for something
else, i.e., as signs of properties of perceived things and events.
The matter looks different only in the comparatively problematic
borderline-case where one seeks to determine the "An-sich"
(pure given-ness) of these qualities in perception" [13].

It is, of course, exactly this "borderline case", namely, the
problem whether conditions for the isolation of the "An-sich"
– given-ness of perceptual data can be instituted or not (and
how such isolation is to be interpreted) that is at issue. The
question, in other words, is whether perceptual data can be
stripped of their various representative functions or not. The
relevance of having recourse to empirical investigations involves
the mere technical possibility of accomplishing such a reductive
stripping of the sensory data. To illustrate the feasibility of that
reduction, Cassirer mentions experiments undertaken by the
German physiologists Helmholtz, Hering and Katz. In his *Aufbau
d. Farbwelt*, Katz had described a procedure involving, a.o., the
observation of colors through a punctured screen. "It turned out
that thereby (the colors) change their phenomenal character and
that there takes place a reduction of the color-impression to . . .
the dimension of plane- (Flächen-) colors" [14].

Hering performed similar reductions by means of a "vision
tube" (eine irgendwie fixierte Röhre), whereas Helmholtz, more

ingenious yet, gets along without any instruments and achieves comparable effects by "looking from upside down, from under one's legs or arms". Thus, Hering: "Place yourself near the window, holding in your hands a piece of white and a piece of grey paper closely together. Now, turn the grey paper towards the window, the white one away from it, so that the retinal image of the grey paper will be more strongly illuminated than the white one; but even though one will notice the change in light-intensity, the now 'lighter' but actually grey paper will still appear as grey, while the now 'darker' but actually white paper will be seen as white. If now both papers are looked at through a tube, one will soon see both papers (if held so that one will not shade the other) as on one and the same level, and now the grey paper will be seen as the lighter one, and the white paper as the darker one, corresponding to the two light-intensities" [15]

· And Helmholtz: "We know that green plains appear, at a certain distance, in somewhat different color-tones; we get used to abstract from this change and we learn to identify the different 'green' of distant lawns and trees with the corresponding 'green' of these objects when seen at close range .... But as soon as we put ourselves into unusual circumstances, when we look, e.g., from under our arms or legs, the landscape appears to us as a flat picture ... Colors thereby lose their connection to close or distant objects and now face us purely in their qualitative differences" [16].

Now, it appears that, if examples of the above type are taken as evidence for the fact that the severing of sensory data from representative contexts is not only possible but actually (technically) achievable, Cassirer would both be proving too much (with respect to what can be maintained within his own strictures) and also not enough (with respect to what he presumes to prove). For one: to suggest that Helmholtz', Hering's and Katz' investigations succeeeded in a "de facto" isolating of the "pure color-phenomena" from their "representative" function would be to maintain more than Cassirer himself could allow for, after having taken pains to point out that the sensory moment can never actually be encountered in isolation from a "sense" (or contextual-) moment. To accept such isolation as a "fact" would certainly not be compatible with his contention that "there is

nothing in consciousness without thereby also being posited ...
something other and a series of such others. For each singular
content of consciousness obtains its very determination from
consciousness as a whole which, in some form, is always
simultaneously represented and co-posited by it" [17]. Nor
could, or need, the above empirical illustrations prove that this
is not the case. What they would seem to support is not the view
that color-values can be 'abstracted' from their representative
function, but only that, by appropriate shifts from a "normal"
perception perspective to a controlled two-dimensional perspective, different interpretations hold with respect to color-phenomena. These have, in effect, not really been stripped of their
"representative" office, but they now represent plane-instead
of surface- colors. That this is the more desirable way of stating
the matter is suggested by an earlier pronouncement: "(After)
the complete reduction of the color-impressions, they do not represent ... a particular thing ... (but) appear as members of a
series of 'light-experiences' (Lichterlebniss). But even these
'light-experiences' betray a certain structure insofar as they are
sharply contrasted with each other, and in that they are organized in that contrast. Not only do they have different degrees of
coherence, so that one color appears separated from the other
by a larger or smaller distance (wherefrom issues a determinate
principle of their serialization), but there are assumed in this
series certain privileged points around which the various elements
can be grouped. Even when reduced to a mere 'light-impression',
the individual color-nuance is not just 'present' as such, but it
also is representative. The individual 'red', given here and now,
is given as 'red', as a member of a (color) species which it represents ... Without this (coordination to a series), the impression would not even be determinable as 'this one' in the Aristotelian sense" [18].

We must conclude, therefore, that on Cassirer's own view it
becomes impossible to conceive of the sensory moment of the
symbol-concept as isolable from any context, structure or series.
Whereas, under specifically controlled conditions, color-, sound-
and other sensory data may indeed cease to function representatively for esthetic qualities, thing-surfaces and shapes or for
conventional language-signs, their "reduction" will still not go

beyond what Cassirer variously calls the "simple perception-experience" (das schlichte Wahrnehmungserlebniss) or the "impression"-level on which they are identifiable as of a determinate "nuance", pitch, intensity. Structure ("serial coordination") will thus be encountered on the perception-level as well as on any other one. Marc-Wogau's charge that the "material" moment of the symbol-concept cannot be conceived of as different from its "formal" (sense-)moment would, accordingly, not only hold but it would also agree with Cassirer's own formulations, if, and only if, the symbol-concept allowed of application in only one "sense"-context. To be sure, within any one perspective, the "whatness" (data) of a phenomenon is never given in separation from its "how-ness" (perspective), the "seen" is not independent from modes of "sight". With a variety of symbolic perspectives, sights, and contexts, however, there is also given the possibility of contrasting and distinguishing them as differently oriented "modes of sight" of which it can be said that they are "of" sensory data in the sense that a reduction to the psycho-physiological context can be performed for all of them.

When Cassirer insists, therefore, that "there is always a world of optical, acoustical and tactual phenomena in which and by means of which all 'sense', all apprehending, comprehending, intuiting and conceiving alone is manifest" [19], then his insistence that a sensory-dimension can always be distinguished from the many sense-perspectives which may be taken of it, must be interpreted to mean that a (psycho-physiologically describable) perception-context can be coordinated to all other contexts in which the senses represent different types of (expressive, intuitional, conceptual) sense.

The "material" moment of the symbol-concept, we could say, as reference for, and "embodiment" of, the sense-endowing "formal" moment, may not be separately encountered or isolated within one context, but it is nevertheless distinguishable as one context itself. To speak of it as "material" would be justified if one takes this term to stand – in the Aristotelian sense, e.g., – for what is taken as that of which manifold determinations are possible. In support of our belief that this interpretation of the "independent variability" of the two symbol-moments is adequate with respect to what Cassirer aims to maintain, let us turn,

in conclusion, to an illustration adduced by him on various
occasions. Cassirer bids us to think of a black line-drawing, a
"Linienzug", given as a "simple perception-experience": "Yet,
while I still follow the various lines of the drawing in their visual
relations, their light and dark, their contrast from the background, their up and down movements, the lines become, so to
speak, alive. The spatial form (das Gebilde) becomes an aesthetic
form: I grasp in it the character of a certain ornament ... I can
remain absorbed in the pure contemplation of this ornament, but
I can also apprehend in and through it something else: it represents to me an expressive segment of an artistic language, in
which I recognize the language of a certain time, the style of an
historical period. Again, the "mode of sight" may change insofar
as what was manifest as an ornament is now disclosed to me as a
vehicle of a mythico-religious significance, as a magical ... sign.
By a further shift in perspective, the lines function as a sensory
vehicle for a purely conceptual structure-context ... To the
mathematician, they become the intuitive representation of a
specific functional connection ... Where in the aesthetic sight,
one may see them perhaps as Hogarth beauty-lines, they picture
to the mathematician a certain trigonometric function, viz., the
picture of a sin-curve, whereas the mathematical physicist
may perhaps see in this curve the law of some natural process,
such as, e.g., the law for a periodic oscillation" [20].

All depends here upon what is taken to remain "identical" in
all these modes of sight. When we say that it is the "line-drawing"
which figures as the "material" moment in all contexts, in which
sense can we say that it is the "same" one, since it is seen as so
many different things from context to context? In the just-quo-
ted passage, Cassirer speaks of the "simple perception experience"
in which the line-drawing is given before it "becomes, so to speak,
alive", i.e., enters into the various contexts. But clearly, if experienceable at all, this "simple perception experience" has its
own contextual "sense" and cannot designate a moment prior
to all contextual sense-making.

Commenting upon the "line-drawing"-illustration, Cassirer
has later on [21] forestalled what, otherwise, would indeed have
constituted a serious inconsistency with respect to the "material"
or perception-mode of the symbol-concept. He points out that

"the material moment is not a psychological datum, but rather a liminal notion (Grenzbegriff) ... What we call the "matter" of perception is not a certain sum-total of impressions, a concrete substratum at the basis of artistic, mythical or theoretical representation. It is rather a line towards which the various formal modes converge. (Eine Linie ... in der sich die verschiedenen Weisen der Formung schneiden). This rather space-metaphorical version of the issue, we suggest, supports our interpretation (p. 83) insofar as the "matter of perception" qua "convergence of the various formal modes" is indeed definable as the "reducibility" of all contexts to the psycho-physiological one from which Cassirer's actual evidence is concededly derived. (Helmholtz, Hering, Katz, etc.)

We conclude from the preceding discussion that a consistent meaning can be assigned to Cassirer's symbol-concept. Its extreme generality is manifest when we express it as a propositional function. We could say that the property of "sensory data representing sense (meaning)" limits in no way whatever the range of the particulars which may enter the argument as true values. A symbolic relation, in other words, must hold for all facts because no facts are held to be stateable without reference to some context; and no context can fall outside the range of the symbol-concept because, as a context, (Sinnzusammenhang), it must establish some exemplification of a representative relationship. This representation of "sense" through the "senses", as was indicated, can take three distinct modal forms:

(1) If the perspective is determined by the emotive-affective interests of man, the senses are said to make "expressive sense".

(2) If the perspective is determined by the volitional-teleological interests of man, the senses are said to make "intuitional" or thing-perceptual sense.

(3) If the perspective is determined by the theoretical interests of man, the senses are said to make conceptual- or scientific sense.

It is to each of these "modi" of the symbolic relation of representation that there correspond the various cultural media. Thus:

(1) The expression-modus is said to be exemplified in the

domains of myth, art and (the sub-strata of) language,
wherever we deal with what Cassirer calls "expression-
characters" (Ausdruckscharaktere) and what are referred
to by other contemporary philosophers, in related con-
notations, as "tertiary qualities", "essences", "prehensions", "significant forms", etc.

(2) The intuition- (or thing-perceptual, empirical) modus is
said to be exemplified in the "natural world-view" of
commonsense, both constituted and reflected by language.

(3) The conceptual (or theoretical) modus is said to be exemplified by the order-systems of signs in which we have
the world of science.

The philosophy of symbolic forms hereby becomes a philosophy
of cultural forms, since it is from them alone that one can read
the various modalities of symbolic world-perspectives, the multi-
form directions of representations which define the range of the
symbol-concept.

From these cultural exemplifications of the "modi" of the
symbol-concept, we must distinguish its "qualities", i.e., the
pervasive relations of space, time, cause, number, etc., said to be
"constitutive" of any and all objectivity. No matter how differently, in other words, perception functions to represent to us the
meaningful worlds of myth, art, common sense and the sciences,
none of these variously oriented types of reality-accounting will
be found to lack some of the most pervasive symbolic relations
in their spatial, temporal, causal and numerical organizations.
But since each of these constitutive relations is never manifest
but in one of the three specified modal forms: "we may conceive
certain spatial forms (e.g., lines) as an artistic ornament in one
case, as a geometrical draft in another ... so that, in consequence,
the quality of a relation can never adequately be given except in
reference to the total system from which it is abstracted. If, e.g.,
we designate the temporal, spatial, causal, etc. relations as
R_1, R_2, R_3 ... there belongs to each of these a special 'index of
modality' u_1, u_2, u_3 ... which indicates the context within which
they are to be taken" [22]. It follows that Cassirer could not consider adequate any philosophical analysis of space, time, cause,
number, etc., unless, besides paying attention to mathematical
and physical spaces, it also attempted to account for the ex-

pressive and intuitional "spaces" of common sense, art, myth and religion.

We must, therefore, try, in a subsequent chapter, to come to an understanding of what Cassirer means by the "symbolical" nature of these pervasive, "constitutive" relations and what benefit accrues to an examination of them, if followed through the three modal forms of symbolic representation.

CHAPTER V

THE MODALITIES OF THE SYMBOL CONCEPT

(*Space in Myth, Perception and Science*)

Upon defining and considering objections as well as a possible defense of Cassirer's symbol-concept, we have come to the conclusion that it formulates, on a level of highest generality, the thesis that neither sense-data nor thought by itself can account for those peculiar and specifically organized forms in which, as a matter of cultural fact, we alone can experience "reality" in its various mythico-dramatic, perceptually pragmatic and theoretical-scientific aspects. This tenet of the philosophy of symbolic forms, namely that in all dimensions of experience-accounting we can, upon analysis, distinguish differently oriented perspectives, types of "synthesis", directions of "sight" as so many forms of evaluating and interpreting the phenomenally given "data of sense", in Cassirer's opinion, can be made especially clear in the case of the "spatial organization" of reality which, to common sense, appears as one of its most immediate, non-mediated and non-symbolic features. He argues that relations of proximity and togetherness (Mit-und Beieinander), of here-, there- and between-ness, while apparently as independent of an interpreting observer as the given phenomena among which they hold, are recognized, upon reflection, to be intelligible only as rather complex and mediated products of symbolic representation. In attributing a certain size, position, or distance to any kind of object, we are not asserting "properties" of sense-data, but relations holding for the phenomena considered. Cassirer takes it as a secured result of both epistemological and psychological analyses of space that any organization "within" it does presuppose types of "judgments" and "evaluations" of the perceptually given data of sense. In support of this contention, let us briefly review two philosophical sample-analyses of space, characteristic of rationalist and empiricist types of analysis.

Descartes

The procedure by which Descartes arrives at the notion of an "extended substance" after having rendered illusory all such "secondary" qualities as color, sound, solidity, etc., has by now become a classic of rationalistic reduction. Two aspects of his analysis are important to note: 1) the concept of material "substance" is defined by him in terms of its spatial characteristic of extension only, and 2) neither "substance" nor its extensional thing-manifestations are conceived as being given directly and immediately in perception. "Sight affords us but images, hearing only sounds; it is evident, therefore, that this 'something' of which we think as what is signified by these images and sounds, could not come to us through our senses" [1]. For Descartes, the features both of our "intuitive" and the more rigorous "geometrical" space are of a "rational" character. Neither position, size and distances nor continuity, uniformity and infinity are revealed to man through any of his five senses. Spatial determinations are "estimated" or "calculated"; they involve acts of measurement and thus become subsumable under the deductive method of Descartes' "mathesis universalis".

Berkeley

Berkeley, in his *New Theory of Vision*, shares one of Descartes' convictions: spatial organization cannot be grounded upon the mere occurrence of perceptions. For the philosopher of extreme "sensationalism", as for Descartes, "space" cannot arise with, or reside in, the perceptions themselves, nor can it be understood as a peculiar sort of perception which, somehow, accrues to the complex of the "legitimate" perceptions. If we perceive our perceptions to be in "space", we do so by virtue of complex processes of interpretation and "comparison". Such "comparisons", however, are not determined by the type of geometrical rules which Descartes had invoked earlier. The latter's space of "pure extension", as well as Newton's "absolute space", are to Berkeley so many idols rather than ideas. It is "perversion to give sight to man through geometry" [2]. For evidence that spatial organization is neither immediate not the outcome of strictly geometrical rules,

Berkeley goes back to the famous question, asked by Molyneux
(in his *Optic*) and mentioned in Locke's *Essay*. Molyneux had
posed the following question: suppose a man, born blind, was
made to see after an operation, what theretofore he had only had
occasion to touch. Will this man recognize the newly disclosed
optical perceptions as belonging to the same object of which he
previously had tactual perceptions only? Will both kinds of
perceptual data be referred to one and the same thing? Berkeley
answers this question in the negative; he sees no "necessity" to
connect the quite dissimilar sensations of touch and sight, of pres-
sure-resistances and light-impressions. If these otherwise hetero-
geneous classes of perceptions are eventually coordinated for
the realization of spatial organization, it is not because of any
inner logicality or necessity, but simply because of the "suggesti-
bility" of the self by virtue of which perceptions may mutually
signify or touch each other off. It is this power of "suggestion",
grounded on habit rather than a deductive system, which best
accounts for the circumstance that some perceptions can "signify" others with respect to their size, distance or location.

As regards early psychological "explanations" of spatial experience, they either confined themselves to providing corrobor-
ative evidence for either one of these two main philosophical
alternatives, or, as in Helmholtz, they represent an attempt to
combine both Cartesian intellectualism and Berkeleyan empiricism in a theory of "unconscious inferences". For Helmholtz, the
integration of sense-impressions within a spatial order is relegated
to associative laws of connection and "reproductive functions"
of the imagination for the study of which he had to found an
entirely new science: physiological optics. It was Hering's "na-
tivistic" space-theory, however, which impressed both Cassirer –
and W. James earlier – as a more promising approach to the problem. "No artfulness of a psychological chemistry (of the type so
skillfully wielded by Helmholtz) has ever succeeded in actually
solving the mystery of the genesis of a space-consciousness" [3].
Contemporary psychologists seem to have shared his reservations
regarding all attempts to explain the "spatial" in terms of a construction from elements which are in principle non-spatial. The
hope to catch somehow the acts by which sense-"impressions"

become "space-perceptions" seems to have dimmed for all interested parties. Modern analyses emphasize as factual an examination as possible of the moments (learning-processes) which can be experimentally isolated from given space-perceptions and thus can be evaluated as different "conditions" for its occurrence [4]. More recently, topological psychologists (Kurt Lewin and followers) have called attention to a "social space", at once (psychologically) more immediate and yet more clearly mediated by symbolic relations of social, and socially learned, differentiations. According To J. F. Brown, "the chief difference between the psychological field and the physical field is that direction and magnitude of the point values within the field are not as yet to be given with the same precise definition ... The non-metrical dynamical concepts which we will use are fluidity, degree of freedom of social locomotion, permeability, tension and vector ... In general (e.g.), the degree of freedom of social locomotion varies inversely with the number of barriers within the field" [5]. This quotation may just suffice to suggest the use to which space-terminology could be put when applied to directions, distances and motions within a "social space". Sociometrics has since demonstrated both the cognitive fruits of social space – thinking and also its limitations.

What matters, for our purpose, is that without the recognition of social determinants of perception we should be in no position to account for differences in the space-interpretations upon otherwise similar sensory cues. If sensory perception were really just a matter of neuron vibrations of the optic nerve and impulse-transmissions to the occipital cortex, space-perception would indeed appear to be a purely "individual" phenomenon. But, as O. Kleinberg put it, "considerable evidence has accumulated ... which indicates that social factors must be considered if the phenomena of sense perception are properly to be understood" [6].

In a much-quoted report of a well-conducted experiment [7], Sherif found that individuals, reporting on point-movement observations (in a dark room), offered different protocols when tested in isolation but tended to converge when reporting under conditions of group-testing and opportunity for communication. When re-tested, individuals tended to retain group judgments on what was "seen" rather than their pre-collective perception reports, thereby suggesting laboratory evidence for the general assumption of cultural patterning of color- and space perceptions, as it was entertained by Malinowski, Seligman, Mead and many others on the basis of anthropological data.

In view of the growing success of experimental and comparative methods in the isolation of conditions that mediate space-perception, one may wonder what could still be expected from a philosophical concern with this issue. Is there any other method, known only to the philosopher, that could add anything to the scientific analysis of the space-problem? Does it even make sense to speak of a space "problem" now that scientists have finally succeeded in resolving it into experimentally isolable components?

To be sure, the philosopher will not compete with the experimental scientist in the determination of those factors and combinations of factors which either genetically explain the "coming about" of space-experience, causally determine its "conditions", or phenomenally describe its features. According to Cassirer, there remains one aspect of the problem which is relevant for the philosopher: by virtue of which acts of "mediation" or "symbolic representation" can the experience of "spatiality" become a vehicle for the entirely different space-structures of myth, the natural world-view, art, geometry, physics, etc?

One final reservation may be voiced – and answered – here before we shall turn to Cassirer's actual space-analyses: admitting that the philosopher be right in his insistence that, beyond psychological investigations, other inquiries have bearing on a full understanding of the space-concept, what exactly will be his task? While he may be commended for being mindful of the variety of space-forms, he can hardly be said to either have initiated or much less to be in a position to settle the whole conspectus of space-theoretical subject-matter as it has evolved in the various mythological, esthetic, psychological, mathematical and physical investigations. Unless the philosopher is to add to the number of all those spatial organizations a special, philosophical "space" of his own, it would seem that the only other choice he has would be to offer some sort of "interpretation" or "integration" of the spaces of art, common sense, science, etc., or simply to consider these as illustrations for a more comprehensive and all-embracing definition of the space-concept.

Our preceding discussion will already have suggested that Cassirer holds both that spatial relationships characterize all types of experience-accounting and also that no space-analysis is philosophically adequate unless it can allow for the multi-dimensionality of space-conceptions as they have culturally been worked out. But why, one may ask now, should this "multi-dimensionality", this great variety of space-forms, be reducible to what we already know will be only three – and not more than three – modalities (expressive, intuitional and theoretic) of symbolic representation? With what right would such a scheme legislate as to the number of "types" under which all culturally extant space-forms will be subsumable? Such a three-fold division, to be sure, would have been as startling to earlier philosophers (with their two-fold division of intelligible- and imaginary-, real- and illusory-spaces) as it would appear to conflict with more recent realizations of a far greater variety of spaces. Thus, we have become accustomed by now to think that there are as many conceptual spaces as there are geometricallly interpretable axiom-sets. Psychologists have familiarized us with differently centered "action-spaces". Bees, ants and other social animals are said to live in "'social" or "pragmatic" spaces. In addition, art-historians (Woelfflin, Green) and culture-historians (Spengler) have warned us that, unless we learn to think in different "space-feelings" or "culture-spaces", we will be unable to come within emotional range of the major style epochs. "When we talk of style today, we are all thinking more or less in the same style, just as we are all using the same languages, whether we are considering mathematical space or physical space, or the space of painting or that of actuality, although all philosophizing that insists ... upon putting an identity of understanding in the place of such kinship of significance-feeling must remain somewhat questionable. No Hellene, Egyptian or Chinese could re-experience any part of those space-feelings of ours and no art-work or thought-system could possibly convey to him unequivocally what space means for us" [8].

Instead of imposing a three-fold scheme, would it not be more sensible, in the face of this situation, either to single out one space-form as more reliable, exact or "real" than the others, or to make up one's mind to accept them all? I think it is important to understand here that, if Cassirer bids the philosopher to go beyond such mere "acceptance" to an inquiry into the modal forms of symbolic representation, he is not thereby asserting anything about the number of possible "spaces". While the philosopher cannot afford to be dogmatic as regards the diversity and number of spatial organizations, as a philosopher he is not done unless he attempts, on a level of higher generality, to account for this variety of organization by making those necessary assumptions (be it about reality or reason or man as the "homo symbolicus") as could make intelligible both the universality and the modifiability of spatial order in human experience.

That an adequate account of this issue can be given in terms of the three distinguishable ways in which sense-data may represent (signify) either emotive, intuitional or theoretic meaning is never argued for by Cassirer as a conclusion, reached by valid reasoning, from unquestionable axioms or data. Philosophical accounts, like the scientific ones on a somewhat lower (and more readily controlled) level of generality, are suggested by the subject-matter which alone confirms and determines the warrant of all and any theoretical accounts. In our subsequent examination of Cassirer's space-interpretations, we shall therefore take care to present his own thought in close connection with the mythological, psychological, linguistic and mathematical references which are offered as providing evidence for the adequacy of the three-fold modality of the symbol-concept in particular and the "symbolic" interpretation of space in general.

THE SPACE OF MYTH

Spatial organization on the expression-
level of symbolic representation

The evidence from which the philosopher may proceed for an estimate of the type of spatial organization encountered, at some time, by all men and, at all times, by some men (the child and the poet), is not limited, as has sometimes been supposed, to descriptive accounts of feeling- and behavior-patterns of the "savage", brought back by the exploring traveller to his civilized contemporaries. For Cassirer, the "primitive" mind and its mode of space-experience can be read more reliably from whatever records we have of its languages, its rituals and artistic creations. It is through these that "myth" articulates its own specific "world" and that an interpretation of its "structure" must be gleaned.

Two presuppositions are implicit here: 1) that there is indeed a "structure" to the proverbially mixed-up phenomenon of myth, and 2) that the philosopher who, since Herakleitos, (and by definition), must have freed himself of all traces of its "illusions", nevertheless is fit both to comprehend and to render "intelligible" its characteristic thought-motives.

As regards the problem of "structure" in myth: Cassirer appears to credit the success of his interpretation with transforming the general assumption that there is such structure into a realization of the specific structure which he discloses as clearly inherent in mythical productivity (*respectively* the records we have of it); and similarly he never questions the "intelligibility" of myth because he evidently felt that the very fact of his finding a plausible interpretation would dispose of the question as a pseudo-problem. In addition, however, one must keep in mind Cassirer's agreement with Hegel on this point (as he expressed it, e.g, in the preface to the third volume of his *Philosophie der Symbolischen Formen*): "For Hegel, the phenomenology becomes the basic presupposition of all philosophical knowledge because he demands of the latter that it comprise the totality of all spiritual forms and because, according to him, this totality cannot be made visible except in the passage of one form into the other ... In this principle, the philosophy of symbolic forms agrees with Hegel – regardless of how differently it must proceed in the realization of this task. But this philosophy, too, intends to illumine the path which leads from the primary forms ... to the forms of theoretical knowledge" [9].

(*1*) *Linguistic Evidence for Spatial Structure in Myth*

In support of the thesis that spatial distinctions are worked out in primitive languages in impressive complexity and detail, Cassirer refers to the studies of men like Boas (Kwakiutl), Westermann (Sudan), Gatschet (Klamath), Crawfurd (Indian) and Codrington (Melanesian). Let us look at just one illustration: according to F. Boas, e.g., [10], a sentence of the type "The man is sick" can only be expressed by means of additional linguistic signs that must co-designate whether the "subject", asserted to be sick, is far or close from the speaker who makes the assertion, or from the listener to whom it is made; reference will also invariably be made of the place, position and posture of the sick man. The point of this – as of a host of similar examples – is to stress both the complexity and conciseness of spatial determinations on the level of myth. By comparison, all other types of discrimination appear undeveloped and weak, unless, indeed, they themselves are expressed, indirectly, through the metaphorical use of space-words.

Suppose the type of evidence, illustrated by just one example above, is accepted as sufficient to support Cassirer's thesis that there is both a complex articulation of space-experience on the level of myth and that its structure is so highly developed that it subsequently was used to express linguistically other, non-spatial, relations through the medium of space-predicates. If this be a fact, born out by anthropological and linguistic evidence, what is its relevance for the philosopher? Cassirer, I think, would have at least two answers to this question. He would point out that, for one, "facts" of this kind are of crucial significance because they do indicate the presence of structure, organization and linguistic determination on a level which philosophers for a long time have looked upon as a "blooming, buzzing confusion" for which only science and philosophy constituted alternatives of "order". More specifically, however, Cassirer would remind us that the mere factuality of exacting mythical space-discrimination would only raise the question of its "possibility", i.e., the realization of the conditions which language must satisfy to function as an agency of the spatial organization of experience. How, indeed, can it so function?

In Cassirer's opinion, there is vast evidence to the effect that in most diverse language-families almost identical sounds (auditory symbols) are employed to accompany almost identical indicative gestures in designating basic spatial distinctions. Both vowels and consonants, it can be shown, provide, in characteristic modifications of quality and pitch, a universal medium through which distance and directions in space can be sharply expressed. Child-psychologists, more recently, have called attention to the fact that the first "lull-words" of baby-talk show a clear distinction between two differently signifying consonant-groups, of essentially "centripetal" and "centrifugal" meanings respectively, with "m" and "n" sounds having an "inward"-reference and the more explosive "p-b" – and "t-d" – consonants having "outward"-reference.[11]. The basic spatial meaning-content of these two sound-groups is also manifest in the earliest demonstrative pronouns as developed in a great variety of (Indogermanic) language types. Characterizations of spatial position, of closeness or distance, i.e., all spatial "sense" is represented by a simple shift from one (sensory) sound-group to another. Thus, the dull vowels (u, o) invariably express the place of the person addressed: you, vouz, tu, du, dort, etc. The sharper vowel-group will use "i" and "e" sounds to indicate proximity of or to the speaker: je, I, ich, ici, here, hier, etc.

Linguistic meaning-variations prior to any semantically-deliberate meaning assignments have been called "phonetic symbolism", and were described by Jespersen and Sapir in by now classic works. More recently, S. S. Newman found that, when asking individuals of different language-habits to range different vowels according to the relative size suggested by them, "i" was the smallest, with "e" following and "ae", "a", "u" and "o" denoting ever larger sizes[12]. Even the extraordinarily cautious Franz Boas, not committing himself to the thesis that all languages will use i d e n t i c a l phonetic elements for space-discriminations, adduces illustrations from Indian languages in support of the theory that "undoubtedly the particular kind of synthesia between sound, sight and touch has played its role in the growth of language"[13]. What matters here is that anthropologists have come to see, (as have linguists and social psychologists), that there is linguistic meaning which precedes the establishment of rules of designation and that, as it were, sounds themselves have meaning. But how can this be? If, on Cassirer's view, there can be no meaning outside of some context of symbolic representation, pre-semantically, sounds must be meaningful in some other context rather than "by themselves".

Sounds, instead of representing words, could represent other sensory experiences, by "synthesia", as Boas thought, or by F. Mauthner's suggestion of kinesthetic sensations arising from the size of the oral cavity: "If we are in a foreign country and, not knowing its language, want to express bigness, we shall open our arms wide; if the opposite, we shall press the palms of our hands together. Now suppose the vocal apparatus desired to share in the gesture; suppose the glottis and the mouth pressed themselves together to articulate an "i" in imitation of a small space, or opened wide into an "o" to imitate a big one" [14].

The above is reproduced merely by way of illustrating the sort of account which could, in principle, explain the pre-semantic meaningfulness of sounds, not by claiming that they have meaning "by themselves" but that they can occur in (synesthetic or kinesthetic) contexts other than semantical ones. There are, to be sure, other spatial discriminations than size and distance. To express them, language must go back to some familiar scheme in analogy to which it may strike out to discriminate less familiar relationships. A study of a number of primitive languages reveals that most other spatial distinctions are made in analogy with the human body which, a familiar and rather universal organization of parts, becomes the reference-scheme for further spatial structuralizing. Once man obtained a sufficiently discriminating conception of his own body, he then had indeed a model in terms of which the rest of his world could become ordered and fixed in language. The 'inner' and 'outer', the 'above' and 'below', the 'before' and 'behind' can verbally be designated only by pre- or post- propositional use of expressions which actually stand for parts of the human physiology. To let one illustration stand for many: many Negro-languages take their space-prepositional words directly from such substantival terms as "back" for "behind", "eye" for "in front of", "neck" for "above", "stomach" for "within" etc.

So much then for a glimpse at the way in which language, by coordinating different sound-groups to differently experienced event-types, manages to effect a basic space-differentiation and how, in subsequently extending familiar order-schemes to ever more discriminating spatial organization, language becomes the agent which connotes and re-inforces a highly intricate mythical space-concept.

Linguistic evidence also appears to support Cassirer's further contention that language is not only involved in the fixing of spatial discriminations, but that its spatial terminology becomes the model or analogue by which essentially non-spatial differences are linguistically connoted. In an illustration of this feature, Whorf points out that "we can hardly refer to the simplest non-spatial situations without constant resort to physical (space) metaphors. I "grasp" the "thread" of another's arguments, but if its "level" is "over my head", my attention may "wander" and "loose" "touch" with the "drift" of it, so that when he "comes" to his "point" we may differ "widely", our "views" being indeed so far "apart" that the "things" "appear" "much" too arbitrary or even a "lot" of nonsense" [15].

Cassirer's occasional contention that spatial discrimination is at the base of all other distinctions, that "the objective world became intelligible and transparent for language to the extent that it succeeded, as it were, to re-translate it into the spatial" [16], that the primitive mind cannot grasp any distinctions unless it has projected them in analogy to whatever determinations are possible through the spatial metaphor – this contention, while not unplausible in the light of the illustrations given, is too peripheral to our purpose to be either questioned or further documented here.

(2) *The Structure of Mythical Space*

We have looked briefly at some of the evidence for Cassirer's thesis that there is a primitive space-structure and how, through the symbolic medium of language, its basic relations are eventually grasped and expressed. We must now turn to an understanding of the significantly different meaning which attaches to these spatial relations in the world of myth. The illustrations adduced by Cassirer strongly suggest that different emotional, if not dramatic, evaluations attach different accents of significance to the various directions and locations in space. Cassirer speaks in this connection of the mythic, "pervasiveness of feeling" in which are rooted the implicit systems of valuation which, in the last analysis, determine, on a pre-scientific level, all the subtleties and complexities which typify the manner in which the spatial order is felt and named.

The basic division, arising on this "feeling-ground", is between the "Holy" and the "Profane" which, according to Cassirer, goes back to or connects with the different experiences of "Light" and "Darkness". "The development of the mythical space-feeling departs throughout from the opposition of day and night, of light and darkness" [17]. Primitive, as well as Babylonian, Egyptian and Iranian mythologies give ample testimony to the pervasiveness of this division, which, when felt as between the "Holy" and "Profane", gives different "accents" to the fundamental space-directions. North and South, East and West will be charged with distinctly different "feeling-tones": they are divine or hostile, friendly or fertile. The East, as the origin of light, may be "felt" as the source of all life, while the West, where the sun goes down, may become charged with all the terrors of death. Given a thorough knowledge of primitive and ancient mythology, it should be possible, according to Cassirer, to read the mythical "way of life" from the mythical "way of conceiving space".

Cassirer here refers to the work of N. Nissen [18] who had arrived at this view after studying the development of the Roman sacral laws. Nissen suggests that the religious awareness of something "holy" becomes a means of "objectification" when understood as something "outward" and spatially distinct. As a thing becomes "holy", it is segregated and „walled off" from the space around it. Linguistically, this act of "holification" by means of spatial determination is preserved in the Latin "templum" which derives from the Greek "templos" (its root "tem") meaning: "to cut out". What is cut out, delimited, is at first the space devoted to a God, later any section of space, (soil, garden or forest) belonging to a king, hero or chief. This act of "delimitation" also extends to the heavens whose constellations and divisions are related to the "templa" (divisions) of divine effectiveness; it establishes "property" as that around which boundaries may be drawn, and eventually penetrates the realms of social, political and legal relations.

Commenting on these (and related) investigations, Cassirer writes: "One still feels the breath of awe that surrounds from the beginning any idea of a spatial limit" [19]. The "limited" and the "unlimited", the "peiron" and the "apeiron" early enter philosophical speculation as the "determined" and the "undetermined", the "formed" and the "formless", the "good" and the "evil". Mythical space-divisions, then, recur in the later speculative cosmologists. And this whole development is telescoped, in language, by the widening signification of the Latin "contemplari" which began its meaning-career as "spatial delimitation" and eventually came to signify – as "contemplation" – all sorts of mental activity.

If it is the "Holy-Profane" – dichotomy which pervades all spatially significant divisions, it follows that locations and directions within it cannot be defined in intuitional or conceptual terms. Instead, spatial relations will be intimately connected with "powers" or "demons" whose respective spheres of efficiency will be charged with specifically different meanings. The "here" and "there", the "up" and "down", each position and place within it, are experienced as endowed with a special "aura" of feeling. The space of myth is thus not a homogeneous space; geometry cannot symbolically represent it. Instead, it is an organization in which the various spatial positions and distances exhibit definite characters of expressive meaning (Ausdruckscharaktere). Proximity and distance, height and depth, left and right are not realized as mere variables of a sophisticated space-thinking; in the world of myth, they figure as true values, interpreted with reference to given systems of magical significance.

Evidence for this interpretation is abundant; the very thorough studies, devoted to "totemistic" systems in particular, have left no doubt that these systems do not only pertain to the individuals and their social relations to the respective "totems", but that they cover everything, so that, whatever does come within the ken of recognition for primitive consciousness at all, is not really intelligible until related to the system of totemistic divisions. In Cassirer's analysis, this great network of organization, weaving together individual, social and cosmic connections into the context of the most subtly divided totemistic family-relationships, also contains its own grand spatial scheme. And vice-versa: it is in examining the totemistic space-schemes that we also are getting at the very core of this complicated web of social relationships that are tied up with it.

In the mythico-religious world-view of the Zuni Indians, (as described by Cushing) [20] the seven-fold division of the universe

to which correspond all things, dead or alive, appears to be derived from the seven-fold determination of their space-scheme,
with its division into the principal directions of North and South,
East and West, Higher, Lower and "Center". It is in close correlation to this type of space-organization, that all things fall into
their proper classes: air belongs to the North, fire to the South,
earth to the East and water to the West. Analogously: winter belongs to the North, summer to the South, autumn to the East and
spring to the West. Human relationships, activities and profes-
sions, likewise, are subsumed under this scheme: war and warriors
are of the North, chase and hunters are of the West, medicine and
agriculture are of the South and magic and religion are of the
East.

It is perhaps worth noting that we are not given here a peculiar
sort of interpretation for some unusual sort of myth. Cassirer
himself has described a good many more instances of this kind,
and the mythological and anthropological literature to which
he refers abounds in illustrations drawn from totemistic societies
as well as from such early civilizations as the Chinese, Indian
and Graeco-Roman. In all of these mythical "universes", we
encounter a "universality" quite different from the type aimed
at by science. As regards the "scientific universe" (cosmos) it is
constituted by laws which hold among its parts. In a "rational"
space-scheme, the relation between the "whole" and its "parts"
is a functional one: the straight line is constructible from "points",
the plane from "straight lines", three-dimensional bodies from
"planes", according to specifiable rules of procedure. Mythical
space, in contradistinction to the space of geometry, is of a
structure not so derivable from its elements but exhibiting, instead, static relations of mutual inclusion (Innesein und Inneha-
ben). No matter how far we push its partition, we always re-dis-
cover in each of its parts the very form and structure of the whole.
And this form, unlike the mathematical space-concept, is not
composed of homogeneous and structureless elements but it per-
sists, as a magical scheme, throughout all of its parts. All connections within mythical space are thus grounded in a primary
identity, conceived not as a "sameness" of geometrical operations
but as an underlying "sameness" of nature and character.

We conclude, then, that in mythical space there is never just coincidence between "what a thing is" and "where a thing is". The place in which anything resides, the direction it takes, immediately enmesh it in a web of relations that are determined by the magical system in which both space- and life-values are ordered. In brief, the sophisticated geometrical distinction between "position" and "content" is not realized in the space of myth. In this respect, mythical space is as unlike geometrical space, as it is like perceptual space. As Mach had pointed out: "The chief directions of organization: before and behind, above and below, left and right are essentially non-equivalent in the two (optical and tactual) physiological spaces" [21]. (*Erkenntnis und Irrtum*, 334). Just as physiological space is distinguished from metrical space in that its "up and down", "left and right" – directions are not reversible or exchangeable because of the quite different organic responses with which they are experienced, so it is with the directions in mythical space which are experienced as being of different magical-emotive meaning. Regardless of all these differences, however, there is one general function which mythical space-schemes share with perceptual, as well as all metrical, "spaces": they accomplish, on the level of an emotive-expressively experienced world, what geometrical space is credited with performing for the "natural worldview" of perception: both serve as organizing schemes by whose mediation the "manifold of our sense-data" is brought under pervasive meaning-perspectives without which no type of spatial orientation would be conceivable.

THE SPACE OF THING-PERCEPTION
Spatial organization on the intuitional level
of symbolic representation

We have now sketched what, to Cassirer, appeared as the essential traits of the type of spatialization, possible on the dramatic (emotive-expression) level of symbolic representation. We have reproduced some evidence for the purpose of indicating how, on the mythical mode of space-conceiving, positions, distances and directions were expressed and differentiated in terms of qualitatively distinct expressive traits and physiognomic characters; we have noted how the symbolic designations of these spatial dis-

criminations (the space-vocabulary) was derived from the analogical relations known to obtain among the members of the human body. Yet – and with this we concluded our preceding section
– it is essential for Cassirer's thesis that, even on the emotional-
magical-dramatic level, a clearly effective and quite "universal"
scheme of spatialization can be, and has been, obtained. Now, philosophers, as a rule, have paid scant attention to pre-scientific
symbolism. As noted earlier in this chapter, however, both philosophers and psychologists were quick to realize the "mediate" or
"symbolic" structure of what has variously been called the
"empirical", "intuitional" or "perceptual" space (Anschauungs-
raum) of common sense and the "natural world-view". In consequence, Cassirer did not have to go into extensive analyses of the
"intuitional" mode of space-symbolization. In the third volume
of his *Philosophie der symbolischen Formen,* he indicates general
agreement with William James' treatment of space-perception
as given in the *Principles of Psychology.*

Let us summarize the gist of Cassirer's interpretation of "perceptual space": perceptions, we are reminded, are not "of"
space, nor could they be of "things-in-space", unless the "flux"
of our successive sensory impressions were somehow arrested and
"focussed" into the realization of a "simultaneity". Simultaneity
must be assumed when, in effect, we do assign different meanings
to the different moments of the experiential process. As long as
each successive moment of experience is noted only in its relation
to this process, it is given only at this moment and it is just as
"fleeting" as any other successive moment. Relative "stations"
within this flux are inconceivable except on condition that some
of its moments (events) are taken to point beyond their own occurrence to something comparatively persistent with respect to
which various other moments could be viewed as so many of its
"aspects". Just as, in listening to a linguistic sign, we grasp, beyond its quality and pitch, also the "sense" which it conveys,
just so we also manage to perceive "objects in space" to the extent
that the ever-changing sensory moments are not merely taken in
their self-sufficiency and "concretion", but that they are "understood" as signs for those quasi-persistent entities which, to common sense, are "things in space".

"Empirical" space then, as the framework in which "things"

are perceptually given, has to be realized as an "acquisition" rather than a "given"; it comes about only when a representative value is attributed to our perceptions, when some are singled out from among them which can serve as "points of reference" around which spatial orientation may proceed. The further question, namely, what type of perceptions is thus to be singled out as "significant" for spatial orientation, is, of course, an empirical one to which only experimental psychology could supply an acceptable answer. Generalizing upon its early findings, William James had already declared that it is "experience that leads us to select certain (perceptions) from among them to be the exclusive bearers of reality: the rest becomes signs and suggestions of these" [22]. It is known how James defines those perceptions that "experience leads us to select" as perceptions seen in "normal positions" and how a "normal position" is in turn defined by him as one in which: (1) we easiest hold anything we are examining in our hands, (2) as a turning point between all right-hand and all left-hand perspective views of a given object, (3) in which symmetrical figures seem symmetrical and all equal angles seem equal, (4) as that starting point of movements from which the eye is least troubled by axial rotation and (5) by which superposition of the retinal images of different lines and different parts of the same line is easiest produced, and consequently by which the eye can make the best comparative measurements in its sweep [23].

Present-day psychologists may not endorse all of these prescriptions as either correct or sufficient; modern texts will, as a rule, add such other "cues" for the transformation of the two-dimensional retinal image to a spatial depth-perception as: (1) relative size, (2) interposition, (3) linear and aerial perspective, (4) clearness of detail, (5) shadows and relative colors and (6) relative movement.

Cassirer will not be expected to make decisions or to voice preferences for any of these factors considered of primary importance for the development and refinement of perceptual-perspective space. The issue of philosophical relevance concerns, again, the circumstance that, no matter which cues are isolated as being conditions of spatialization, they all imply acts of symbolic representation. To say this is not to assert that, in a material mode of speaking, we have, besides the various sensory data, other, i.e., "symbolic" organs which, somehow, collaborate to bring about a world of perceptual space. Nor would Cassirer want to say that there are "added" to the given, two-dimensional, physiological sense-impressions (on the retina) other "ideal", "symbolic" inferences by which the former become projected into a third dimension. What is pre-analytically given is always the experience of a spatial whole from which, by controlled experimental procedures, certain features (interposition, relative color, perspective, etc.) may be isolated and evaluated for their respective contributions to an organization of "empirical space". It is from these experiments that the philosopher may gain assurance of empirical evidence for the important role of signifying or mediating functions holding among perceptions in any experience of "things in space".

Commenting upon the type of "signification" involved on this level, Cassirer bids us to think of it in analogy to language. Approvingly, he quotes from James [24] "Almost any form in oblique vision may be a derivative of almost any other in primary vision; and we must learn to translate it into the appropriate one of the latter class; we must learn of what optical "reality" it is one of the optical signs. Having learned this, we do but obey that law of economy or simplification which dominates our whole psychic life when we attend exclusively to the "reality" and ignore as much as our consciousness will let us the sign by which we came to apprehend it. The signs of each probable thing being multiple and the thing itself one and fixed, we gain the same mental relief by abandoning the former for the latter that we do when we abandon mental images, with all their fluctuating images, for the definite and unchangeable names which they suggest. The selection of the several "normal" appearances from out of the jungle of our optical experiences, to serve as the real sights of which we shall think, is psychologically a parallel phenomenon to the habit of thinking in words – and has a like use. Both are substitutes of terms few and fixed for terms manifold and vague".

Commenting on this quotation, Cassirer adds that the various sensory images – by virtue of the process described by James – acquire some sort of "transparency": we seem to see "through them" a constant form and size, an object having a constant

color, regardless of its ever-changing surface-colors. Cassirer a-
gain refers to Hering's physiological investigations and his search
for the "mechanism" that would explain the fact that snow and
coal, e.g., would preserve their apparent blackness and whiteness
in full daylight, even though the "absolute brightness" of snow
at twilight was less than that reflected by coal at sunlight. More
recently the "Gestaltist", and their American colleagues who
refined and checked their procedures, have given much attention
to the "constancy-phenomenon". Their work, too, could be taken
by Cassirer as confirming his early conviction that all the various
spatial discriminations of form, depth, position and distance –
as they occur on the most "immediate" level of perceptual experience – turn out, upon closer analysis, as conditioned by
"cues", "signs" or briefly: as representative functions of the kind
which characterize all other forms of symbolization.

The abstract, conceptually-symbolical space of geometry, to be
sure, with its requirements of uniformity, continuity and infinity,
differs markedly from the intuitional -symbolical space of perception. Regardless of all other differences, however, Cassirer emphasizes that both "spaces" share this one trait: they each exemplify
specifically different types of"invariancy". Cassirer admittedly
derives this idea from Felix Klein's *Erlanger Programm* [25], according to which the "forms" of different geometries are declared to
hinge upon specific relations selected as "invariant" within their
respective axiom-sets. We go, in other words, from plane-geometry
to projective-geometry by including, with the various possible
operations with respect to which a figure is considered "invariant"
in plane geometry, other operations which, by definition, were
excluded from it but which are now permissible in projective
geometry. Thus, in plane-geometry, a figure remains "invariant"
regardless of its changes in motion, similarity-transformations or
mirroring operations; in projective geometry other transforma-
tions are compatible with the "invariancy" of the geometrical
meaning of a figure. Each and every geometry may then be taken
as an "Invarianten-Theorie" whose validity is determined with
respect to specific transformational groups.

Taking his cue from here, Cassirer suggests that this manner
of interpreting the various possible geometrical space-concepts
merely carries on a process which, in a less sophisticared manner,

is found to operate already on the level of space-perception. The many psychological and physiological accounts of space-perceptions appear, indeed, to agree on this one point: "things-in-space" are not just passively "received" through various optical impressions. Without "selective grouping" of perceptions, without having some of them represent or signify others, we should have no quasi-invariant "things-in-space". Here, as well as in the construction of different geometries, we can shift "points of reference", select different "centers" as relevant and group all impressions around them in relationships of "representation". Corresponding to such shifts, phenomena will not only assume a different geometrical meaning, but they will also undergo radical changes in their perceptual appearance. Cassirer mentions, in this connection, the phenomena which have been brought together under the heading of "optical inversions". Optical complexes, as was shown by Hornbostel [26], when turned on different planes, will "tumble" from one apparent shape to another. A flat wire-model, if seen from different perspectives, appears as either "convex" or "concave". It is significant here that, when these inversions occur, they happen as single, complete and unified movements; it is not that first one part "tips over" and then another, etc. "These quasi-solid inversions are neither illusory nor ideational constructs ... (they are) things which under special conditions we perceive" [27]. Again, it is the shift in perspective that conditions the manner in which spatial forms are perceived.

There is, at this time, no further argument regarding the dependence of plane-, solid- and projective-"spaces" upon the selection of criteria which we choose to consider as "invariant" with respect to specified operations. Cassirer maintains that it is by comparable acts of selection that we "empirically" perceive "things-in-space". As we single out some positions as "normal", we give privileged status to some sensory impressions above others; as we distinguish "real" (surface-) colors from plane- or space-colors, as we differentiate between "apparent" and "real" distance, etc., we are always, in fact, engaging in so many acts of selection and perspective-taking around which phenomena may be rotated. Angles and directions of such "rotation" may shift, and as they do, optical and other sensory data will represent different spatial properties on the intuitional level of symbolization.

THE SPACE OF GEOMETRY
Spatial organization on the conceptual level
of symbolic representation

In the early phases of geometrical thought, space- and number-concepts are developed in close correlation. We know how Pythagoras "elucidated" relations obtaining among numbers from their "representation" in spatial configurations, an idea which turned out to be as suggestive to Descartes as it proved disturbing to Zeno, whose "apories" rendered such "representation" questionable and led to a clearer separation of the logos of number from the logos of space. Later thinkers have, as a rule, been impressed with the distinctness of these two concepts. Compared with the deductive coherence which holds for the system of numbers, the "order" of space seems to present itself to us as the "given" *per se,* unaffected by rational conventions or constructions. The twentieth-century logification of mathematics has accentuated this difference even more sharply. Thus, Russell, whose aim it had been to derive the number-concept from purely logical constants, acknowledges the hiatus between number- and space-thinking, more precisely, between arithmetic and "applied" geometry. As regards "pure" geometry, on the other hand, it is a "logical construct" as much as the science of number. "Pure" geometry, however, – and this is the point – as an investigation into all (logically) possible space-systems, does not determine in any way the features of "actual" or "real" space. "It was formerly supposed that geometry was the study of the space in which we live ... But it has gradually appeared, by the increase of non-Euclidean systems, that geometry throws no more light upon the nature of space than arithmetic upon the population of the U.S." [28]. "Actual" space, in other words, can only be read from experience.

It is at this point, where "pure thought" seems to have reached its limit, that Cassirer bids us to realize its characteristic function. It is discharged in the elaboration of those order- and measure-systems which, as plane-, metric- and projective geometries, determine different types of spatial organization. None of them

makes any statements about "actual" things in "actual" space.
What they formulate, instead, are "possibilities", "ideal" schemes by which the "actual" may or may not be ordered. The
decision, whether the "actual" will or will not submit to these
"possible" orders, is left to "experience" – we are told. What can
that mean? Surely not that experience, pure and simple, can
furnish principles from which its "possible" spatial order-forms
could be deduced. The role reserved to experience is rather to
select which of the "possible" order-forms will apply or fit its
uses. The deductive systems of pure geometry are on the same
level of logical generality as the system of numbers with which
they compare as "calculi" but from which they differ as "interpretations" Experience, it follows, has no more business in the
establishment of geometrical axiom-systems than it has in the
interpretation of complex numbers. On this, at least, there is
agreement among contemporary philosophers of science.

But if the above holds, if geometrical systems are indeed so
utterly independent of empirical considerations, why can some
of them nevertheless be so successfully applied to the actually
given data of perception? Plato, who first conceived of a strict
separation between the world of figures and numbers (ideas) on
one hand and the Herakleitean "flux of becoming" on the other,
proposed to explain their connection in terms of a "participation"
(metechis). It is just such a "participation" of the empirical with
the mathematical that we have in mind when, in our terminology,
we speak of "coordinating definitions" by which a "pure" syntax
is interpreted as holding for an empirical context. We are thus
lead to an important distinction between the "empirical relevance" and the "formal (systematic) validity" of a geometrical
space-scheme. As regards "the validity of any deduction . . .
(it) cannot depend upon the material interpretation which may
be given to the symbols of the calculus. Expressions are equivalent in a system of pure algebra by virtue of the rules for combin-
ing the elements of the system whatever be the interpretation
which may satisfy them" [29]. As regards the relevance of the interpretation effected, it concerns the selection of elements, ascertainable in empirical experience, which are supposed to exemplify
the prescriptions implied in the calculus. Thus, we could select a
visual phenomenon, such as the propagation of light, as an em-

pirical "analogon" for what, in "pure" geometry, would satisfy the definition of a "straight line". Other "analogues" could be chosen and related to the geometrical system by "coordinating definition". As we shift our decisions with regard to which movements we shall consider "linear" and which bodies "rigid", we shall also have shifted from one geometry to another.

Leibniz has made reference to this "coordinating relation" with noteworthy precision: "While it is true – he argues against Locke – that, in conceiving the body, one conceives of something other than space, it does not thereby follow that there are two "extensions", one of space and one of the body. This is just as in conceiving of different objects at the same time, one conceives of something other than the number, i.e., the numbered objects. And yet there are not two multitudes, one abstract (i.e., in number) and the other concrete (i.e., the numbered objects). One could say in the same way that it is not necessary to imagine two types of extension, one as being abstractly of space, and the other being concretely of the body; the concrete, being what it is only in the abstract". (le concret n'estant que tel que par l'abstrait) [36].

In setting up a connection between the "order of the concrete" and the "order of the abstract", between the symbols of pure geometry and their imperfect realizations in empirical "analogues", it is not required that a single, separate symbol should isomorphically correspond to a single and separate "thing". Coordination may relate a set of symbolic operations on one hand and a determinate empirical context on the other. Considering this (and also the circumstance that it seems to be a rather arbitrary matter whether we "coordinate" an optical phenomenon (light-ray) or a haptic phenomenon (a razor blade) as the empirical meaning to the geometrical meaning of a "straight line") it has sometimes been claimed that the geometer now enjoys a rather boundless freedom in spatially determining the particulars encountered in actual experience. There is an important regulative "check" on his discretion, however: "we must choose those assumptions on the basis of which we achieve a simple and systematically complete explanation of empirical phenomena" [31]. Since both "simplicity" and "completeness" are scarcely ever ascertainable in a definitive sense, it always remains possible, by

appropriate syntactical shifts, to arrive at empirically more
satisfactory results. Cassirer emphasizes throughout that by depriving the mathematical symbols of their claim to "absolute
validity", one is not thereby rendering them "subjective" or
relative to any arbitrary convention. Whatever "objective"
meaning is maintained for them, it is grounded upon the precision and adequacy with which they "order" their analogues in
the empirical world. While there is no "finality" to this "objectifying" process, its direction is nevertheless as determinate
as scientific inquiry itself. Whether its objective is interpreted as
the establishment of a unity of one deductive system of propositions, or of a limited number of such propositions that permit of
semantic coordination to the actual world, it is true that we are
"free" to some extent as regards the symbols and relations we
select, but we are also "bound" with regard to all further steps
prescribed by that choice. "When certain conventions are ar-
bitrarily made about the manipulation of symbols, the consequences of these conventions are not themselves arbitrary or
conventional" [32]. These "consequences" – be they of geometrical
or any other type of conceptual order – require evaluation with
respect to both their "formal validity" within a syntax and
their "empirical relevancy" within a selected semantical coordination. Thus, while we can conceive of a great number of geometrical space-forms, there will be only few of them that could
permit of application to either medium-scale (Euclidean) or
large- and small-scale empirical contexts. But whether geometric-
ally "pure" or "applied", whether interpreted or not, all of them
would be "symbolic" in the sense that, in every case, certain
sensory vehicles (either conventional notations or perceived
point-, line- or body-analogues) "represent" a spatial meaning,
context, order or system. The type of this "representation", as
we have seen, may be of an immediate and "felt" nature, as in
the case of the expressive-magical space of myth; it may be of
an intuitionally-practical nature, as in the case of the "natural
world-view" of thing-perception; or, finally, it may be of a rule-
determined nature, via syntactical rules in the case of all "pure"-
geometrical space-concepts; or via coordinating rules in the case
of the empirically-applicable geometrical space-systems.

It is perhaps unnecessary to admit that we have not tried, in this chapter, to offer a technically satisfactory analysis of emotive, perceptual or geometrical space-concepts. From our selective accounts of Cassirer's manner of treatment it may be possible, however, to derive some idea both as to the range through which he aims to carry the analysis of the space-concept and the ensuing enrichment of the philosophical enterprise if this manner of treatment were to be applied to such other "order-relations" as time, matter, cause, number, etc., which, as the most pervasive features of being (experience), are of that universal and yet specifically modifiable nature upon which philosophical reflection, from its inception, has directed its most ingenious efforts.

CHAPTER VI

SEMIOTIC AND PHILOSOPHY OF SYMBOLIC FORMS

We have, in our first chapter, attempted to sketch what appeared to us as the characteristic attitudes of both rationalistic and empiricist schools of thought in their respective evaluations of the symbolic media of knowledge. In both, we pointed out, there was an either hopeful or painful realization that a great deal, if not indeed all, of human knowledge of reality was of a mediate and symbolic, rather than of an immediate or intuitive (perceptual), nature. At the risk of oversimplification, it could perhaps be said that recent and contemporary philosophy has neither completely shared the rationalist's trust nor the empiricist's distrust, but has, instead, become somewhat resigned to the scientific symbolisms which in our days have so successfully increased the scope of human cognition. With respect to "scientific knowledge", there has, indeed, been hardly a doubt during the last few decades that it is best understood as a great feat of symbolic transformation. Bergson, Whitehead, Russell, Peirce, James, Santayana and Dewey, to name only the great and disregard all differences between them, provide eloquent commentaries for this contention. Hand in hand, however, with this pervasive realization there is also a very definite insistence that the "state of affairs", the "facts" or "reality itself" to which all our symbols and constructions "apply", could not also be of a symbolic nature but something other and more basic than human perspectives, conventions or symbolizations. Faced with the alternative of either having to hold staunchly to an otherwise suspect "commensense" reality or to be stamped as "idealists", philosophers have sought non-symbolic anchoring grounds for the various linguistic and scientific symbolisms of knowledge in immediate intuitions, actual occasions, essences, prehensions or "experiences as had" over against "experiences as reflected upon".

Thus, while the role of symbols for the "intelligibility" of reality is surely not a new discovery and has been realized by philosophers since Herakleitos, we suggest that: (1) the realization of a "symbol-problem" is a more recent event, and (2) it is at this point that Cassirer's agreement with, as well as specific divergence from, other contemporary philosophers is most distinctive.

One cannot start out with a discussion of the symbol-concept without noting how widely scattered is the subject-matter to which it has been applied. It has been remarked, at an earlier period, that the study of epistemology was such a difficult one because it often turned out to be some sort of a "borderland" between psychology and metaphysics. The study or "science" of signs, called semiotic, would seem, by comparison, to lead us into a veritable "no-man's land", with anthropologists, linguists, philologists, mythologists, logicians, mathematicians, physicists, estheticians, "normal"- and "abnormal"-psychologists all roaming about and curiously reluctant to leave, even though, as a rule, they scarcely seem to be interested in each other's company. The philosophical inquiry into sign- and symbol-functions, like the earlier one into "ideas", by having to account for so many usages, is in danger of arriving at generalities so pale that nothing, except possibly the inquirer's own good will at classification, would appear to stand out distinctly. According to Charles S. Peirce, e.g., there are some 50,000 symbol-situations that are distinguishable and reducible to only 66 of them [1].

More recently, Charles W. Morris has made two attempts to systematize the obstreperous flock by taking his principles of division either from the positivistic distinction of pragmatic, semantic and syntactic "dimensions" of meaning [2], or by distinguishing them according to diverse "modes of signifying" (informative, appraisive, evocative, etc.) and "sign-usages" (religious, artistic, scientific, etc.). Critics, while they disagreed on the "security" of his behavioristic "foundations", have, as a rule, not questioned either the scope or the usefulness of Morris' terminology. We shall start, therefore, with a characterization of what he calls a "sign-situation" and develop Cassirer's interpretation in contrast to it.

The meaning of a sign, we are warned at the outset, cannot be looked for anywhere in space and time, as one might look for a marble. It can be discovered only within a process, called "sign-function" (semiosis), formulated as a three-term relation: "The most effective characterization of a sign is the following: 'S' is a sign of 'D' to 'I' to the degree that 'I' takes account of 'D' in virtue of the presence of 'S' " [3]. Here "I" stands for the interpretant of a sign, "D" for what is designated and "S" for the sign-vehicle (written or spoken mark, sound or gesture). In this general form, the proposal to understand the sign-process as one of a "mediated-taking-account-of" is fully consonant with Cassirer's own view. There are some terminological shifts, of course. Morris' "interpretant" would turn into Cassirer's "Geist" or "Bewusstsein" (mind, consciousness): "The meaning (held by a) 'mind' (Geist) is disclosed only in its expression; the 'ideal form' (designated by an expression) comes to be known only in and with the system of sensory signs by means of which it is expressed" [4]. The distinction, furthermore, between the sign-vehicle (S) and its designation (D) is conceived, as with Morris, in strict correlation and called, variously, "the sign and the signified", the "particular and the general", the "sensuous (sensory) and its sense", ("das Sinnliche und sein Sinn). Both Morris and Cassirer agree that for anything to be a sign does not denote a property which qualifies a special class of objects, but that it indicates (in the material mode) that it participates in the sign-process as a whole within which it "stands" to somebody for something, or (in the formal mode) that it can be defined only in terms of a three-term relation "I-S-D-," where 'I' designates the "taking account of" (by mind or interpreter), 'S' the mediating vehicles of such account-taking (signs, signals, symbols) and 'D' the (matter, reference of) "what" is taken-account-of. In Cassirer's language: "The act of the conceptual determination of what is designated (eines Inhalts) goes hand in hand with the act of its fixation by some characteristic sign. Thus all truly concise and exacting thought is secured in the 'Symbolik und Semiotik' which support it" [5].

Agreement goes thus far and not further. For a correct understanding of Cassirer's position all depends on what interpretation we put upon his metaphor of the sign and signified "going hand in hand". For Morris, e.g., the relationship suggested here between sign-vehicle and sign-designation is alternatingly alluded to as one of signs "indicating", "announcing" or "suggesting" the presence of whatever they denote, designate or signify. For Cassirer, on the other hand, Husserl's dictum in the matter holds: "Das Bedeuten ist nicht eine Art des Zeichen-Seins im Sinne der Anzeige". (Signification is not a kind of indicative sign-use) [6].

There is, to be sure, more than a terminological issue involved in Cassirer's emphasis on the "signifying" or symbolic function of signs and the semiotician's preference to treat symbols as a (less reliable) sub-class of signs. As regards the terminological difference, it is somewhat camouflaged by the fact that Cassirer often uses both "signs" and "symbols" interchangeably, while, at other times, he would, like Morris, speak of "symbols" as a specific (conventional) type of sign. A reading of the *Philosophie der Symbolischen Formen* (and its abbreviated English summary in *Essay on Man*) brings out at least these four presentations:

1) All symbols are signs. To avoid repetition, Cassirer often lets the term "Zeichenfunktion" mean the same as "Symbolfunktion".
2) Only signifying (Bedeutung habende) signs are symbolic; indicative (anzeigende) signs are "mere signs".
3) Signs have mere "being" – only symbols have a "function".
4) Signs are fixed – symbols are flexible.

The last two formulations, occurring in the *Essay on Man*, are unhappy ones and must be qualified in the light of Cassirer's actual thought as it emerges more clearly from other passages. Thus, as we found in our examination of the "symbol-concept", it too has "being" (in the sense of existence) just as all signs have; both require "sensory" vehicles, carriers, i.e., physical existents to mediate their "indicative" or "signifying" functions. And vice versa: both signs and symbols have their "functions" – however different these may be. As regards the last statement, namely, that "signs are fixed – symbols are flexible" – it is defensible if one considers natural signs only – whose "fixety" is anchored in the causal, empirical context in which they function. There are, it is true, other signs which, being indicative, are not symbolic, but which yet are flexible rather than fixed, i.e., conventional signals. (A whistle as well as a red light may indicate the coming of a train – and both "signs" may indicate other things as well).

With the above qualifications in mind, we can now come back to the gist of Cassirer's distinctions: the "indicative" function of signs, upon the broad basis of which Morris attempts to ground his "semiotic", is rejected by Cassirer as inadequate for an understanding of the "symbolic" function of signs. The difference between these two "functions" is formulated clearly by John Dewey: "Existent things, as signs, are evidence of the existence of something else, this something being at the time inferred rather than observed. But words, symbols, provide no evidence of any existence. Yet, what they lack in this capacity, they make up for in creation of another dimension ... Clouds of certain shapes, size and color may signify to us the probability of rain; they portend rain. But the word "cloud", when it is brought into connection with other words of a symbol-constellation, enables us to relate the meaning of being a cloud with such different matters as differences of temperature and pressures, the rotation of the earth, the laws of motion, etc." [7]. This distinction between the indicative and the symbolic sign-uses has been further sharpened, with obvious reference to Morris, by S. K. Langer. "(There is) a one-to-one correspondence of sign and object by virtue of which the interpretant, who is interested in the latter and perceives the former, may apprehend the existence of the term that interests him ... The fundamental difference between signs and symbols is this difference of association, and consequently of their use by the third party to the meaning function, the subject; signs announce their objects to him, whereas symbols lead him to conceive their objects" [8].

It is this "distinction in kind", maintained by Langer in agreement with Cassirer's insistence that the symbol function represents a relationship "sui generis", which is reduced by Morris to a mere "difference of degree": "A symbol, he replies to Langer, is on the whole a less reliable sign than is a sign (that is a signal)... Signals being more closely connected with external relations in the environment, (they are) more quickly subject to correction by the environment ... they on the whole "indicate existences" more certainly than do symbols. But since signals too have varying degrees of reliability, the difference remains one of degree ... The difference is not between "announcing" an object in the case of signals and of "conceiving" an object in the case of symbols, but in the degree of absence or presence of the supporting condition under which dispositions to behavior issue in overt behavior" [9].

Now, whether one agrees with Morris that environmental correction through signals is in all contexts more reliable than in purely symbolic procedures (such as calculations, e.g.) one need not argue with him that, once the behavioristic approach is taken, either type of sign-usage may indeed be conceived as a *comparable* (and not radically *distinct*) means by which behavior can be informed in different degrees of reliability. There surely is no prima facie evidence why anything may not function as both a symbol and a sign, or why, what is used as a symbol in one context (e.g., a word) may not function as a sign (for somebody's presence) in another context of behavior. To take signs as related to "dispositions to behavior" is to be primarily interested in the ways in which they come to inform, incite, appraise or direct action. To emphasize, as is done by Cassirer, the symbolic sign-use is to inquire not into what signs "announce" but into the "domain of objectivity" which they "condition" by the "perspective" they imply. In consequence, an inquiry into the symbolic function of signs is not concerned "with what we see in a certain perspective but (with) the perspective itself ... (so that) the special symbolic forms are not indications, announcements, but 'organs' of reality since it is solely by their agency that anything real becomes an object for intellectual apprehension and as such is made visible to us. The question as to what reality is apart from these forms and what are its independent attributes becomes irrelevant here" [10].

In accordance with the three modal senses in which the symbolic-form concept is used (see p. 58 et. al.), to say that "the symbolic forms are ... organs of reality" would be equivalent to asserting the following three theses:

1) No "reality" can be encountered except in the cultural (mythical, artistic, perceptual or scientific) contexts in which objects are experienced, understood or known.

2) No "reality" can be assigned to any object except in reference to the pervasive symbol-relations of space, time, cause, number, etc., which "constitute" objectivity in all domains listed under 1).

3) No "reality" can meaningfully be ascribed to anything without, in whatever form, assuming a relationship of "representation", (expressed in the symbol-concept), which can be abstracted from any context in which a "sensory" moment "embodies" a "sense"- (or meaning) moment to an interpreter.

In two preceding chapters we have attempted to sketch how a pervasive symbol-relation "constitutes" such different realms of reality as mythico-dramatic, perceptually-commonsense and geometrico-conceptual space; we have also tried so to define and defend Cassirer's version of the symbol-concept as to make it adequate to the universal use which he makes of it. It remains, in the subsequent sections of this chapter, to contrast Cassirer's insistence on the "objectifying" office of the symbolic sign-function with the contemporary semiotician's treatment of "signs" on both the semantic and pragmatic dimension of analysis.

THE SEMANTIC DIMENSION OF SIGN-ANALYSIS

Taking our cue from Carnap and Morris, semantics is defined as that branch of semiotic inquiry which is not concerned with the relations of the sign to its interpretant, nor with the intra-systematic relations obtaining among signs in abstraction from use and designation, but exclusively with what signs "designate". "A sign has a semantical demension insofar as there are semantical rules ... which determine its applicability to certain situations under certain conditions" [11]. What signs "apply" to has been termed by Morris variously their "object", "denotation", "designation" or "signification". Some critics have felt that this definition falls short of being concise, others have held that it is amenable to a consistent interpretation. What matters for our purpose is that, quite regardless whether signs "denote" an "existent" or designate a class of them, whether they "signify objects" in the sense of Aristotle's "being" or St. Thomas' "res", the semantical dimension of sign-analysis is determined by this objective: to formulate (in a meta-language) rules of coordination such as will hold between statements in an object-language and their designata in the object-world.

Now, both Cassirer and the semiotician agree in accepting and starting with the "fact" of language, with historically-existent sign-systems. The "origin" of language is not considered a germane philosophical issue by either party. But while Carnap has been interested in formulating quite specific rules holding for designa tion in simplified and constructed "languages", Cassirer sees a "semantical" issue exactly where the semiotical analysis stops. "In semantical systems – says Carnap – we study the relations between the expressions (of a language) and their designata. On the basis of these facts we are going to lay down a system of rules establishing these relations" [12]. The "facts" mentioned here are, of course, the "relations between the signs and their designation". Thus, while semantics involves the making of decisions with regard to which signs are to be assigned (and to that extent it issues into a conventional system of designation), it is also related to factual uses of designation via pragmatics whose task it is to set up empirical rules describing which specific sets of signs are, as a matter of fact, used to designate "objects" or "states of affairs". But if, admittedly, such rules can be formulated, are we not thereby presupposing the existence of determinate "objects" quite independently of the signs which may variously be assigned to them? Obviously, semantic rules of coordination are not identity-relations, the signs are not the objects – and "the objects need not be referred to by the signs" [13]. If, however, we do assume that such "objects" have a meaning determinate enough so as to let one sign rather than another "stand" for them, how is this to be accounted for if one is committed to the general thesis that there can be no determinate meaning to anything but by virtue of semiotic rules? [14].

In other words: we are said to require semiotic rules as a condition for speaking meaningfully of the designata of signs; yet: we cannot even set up the most basic pragmatic relations between signs and the situations (objects) to which they are applicable, unless these situations are already "meaningful" and determinate to the point of permitting the establishment of rules that are to hold between them and given signs. If "meaning" is to be a function of a sign (semiotic) context, how can "pragmatics", as its alleged basis, presume to formulate rules with respect to sign-situations, unless the latter already offer "meaning" on the object-level of designation prior to, and on grounds distinct from, those self-same pragmatic rules which manifestly could not even get started until such meaning had been practically achieved?

To raise this question is not to contest the fact that rules of the pragmatic type may indeed be formulated for specially constructed languages whose designation can unambiguously (or ostensively) be defined. Another issue remains, however: how about those "objects" and "states of affairs" which, in some determinate sense, must "signify" and have meaning of a kind so that semiotic rules, connecting them with linguistic signs and signusers can be "established"? Cassirer's studies of myth and language are to be taken in this connection as developments and illustrations for his thesis that language, long before being "applied" to "objects", offers the very medium through which objectifying discrimination occurs. It "cuts out areas of significance" from among the "sensory manifold". Beyond the conventional level of "attaching" signs to the object-world, we are bidden to recognize a level of "arresting" the perceptual flux by means of a primary "naming activity".

Cassirer's various announcement on language have not always been read as either plausible or consistent. Sometimes, language is said to be an "organ of reality", the medium through which alone thought occurs, differences are fixed and properties noted rather than merely connoted and communicated. At other times, language is to be itself determined or caused in its selectivity by "foci" of willing, feeling or acting. Language, like the Janus-head, is presented as looking in both directions at once; forward, in determining perception and thought by fixing attention upon selected aspects connoted by it; and backwards, as it were, in being itself controlled by needs, purposes or evaluations which "cause language to select certain pre-eminent forms, to dwell on them and to endow them with a particular significance" [15].

Stepping out of this metaphor, we may ask whether a clear meaning can be given to Cassirer's philosophy of language as symbolic form, or whether we may not have to take a hard and fast stand on either one or the other of two alternatives: if language is a function of need or value-orientations, then it is these, and not language, which figure as pragmatically last determinants for different modalities of perceiving, speaking and thinking. If, on the other hand, language functions as that invisible and unconscious medium which pre-determines both perception and thought, it could indeed lay claim to be called an "organ" of reality rather than a variable dependent upon factors external to it.

It can be shown, however, that this seeming inconsistency attaches to Cassirer's occasional presentations of his view rather than to its cogency. For one thing, priority contests as to which came first, purposes or speech, are neither easily nor profitably decided. Logically, to be sure, we have to make a choice. Either language, in one and the same respect, selects or merely reflects what is selected by some dominant focus of interest. In different respects or stages of development, however, language may, and apparently does, exercise both functions. Cassirer's investigations of the myth-making mentality, of the teleological structure of all "practical and theoretical" concept-formation in commonsense- and scientific languages should leave no doubt that he does not hold to a view of a mysteriously autocratic language-power which, in isolation from all other concerns, makes its own un- fathomable divisions within the perceptual flux. By contrast, Cassirer presents language as sensitive to those interests which are touched off by, and thus come to note, whatever it is that eventually receives the stamp of linguistic recognition. In so doing, however, language both reinforces and perpetuates pre- linguistic concerns and responses and thus, as a matter of fact, channels, controls, limits and determines the range of stimuli which will be perceived or interpreted as relevant and "nota- ble" aspects of a linguistically predigested world.

Semioticians must accordingly presuppose a world in which there are "objects" characterized by distinguishable properties. As Cassirer remarks, however: "everything depends on what one means by a "property" and how such properties are supposed to be originally determined. The formulation of general concepts (i.e., rules determining the designative meaning of terms. CHH) presupposes definite properties; only if there are fixed charac- teristics by virtue of which things may be recognized as similar or dissimilar ... is it possible to collect objects which resemble each other into a class. But, we cannot help asking at this point, how can such differentiae exist prior to language? Do we not rather realize them only be means of language, through the very act of naming then? What causes language to select ... certain pre-eminent forms, to dwell on them and to endow them with a particular significance"? [16].

It is in answers to questions of this type that a philosophy of symbolic forms would have to come into its own. According to Cassirer, we must pay attention to the various directions of "noting", the "perspectives" within which some properties rather than others become visible, before any conscious formulation of denotative or designative rules will be intelligible.

This point could be put more concisely. Strictly speaking, it is not the philosopher who, on his own, is likely to "pay attention" to the manner in which different languages either reflect or reinforce the perspectives from which, for given speech communities, some rather than other aspects of reality will come within view. As a matter of fact, this sort of inquiry, barely begun when Cassirer took note of it, has been carried on by psychologists (experimental, social and clinical), anthropologists, linguists and even sociologists, with results which converge impressively towards Cassirer's early thesis that the perceptual selectivity, fixed and perpetuated by language, was neither intelligible as a reproductive function (copying an already preformed reality-organization), nor as a matter of deliberate semantic assignment. Instead, it is to be understood as a variable dependent upon basic foci of interest, purposes and evaluations. Experimentalists, as a matter of fact, look upon "selection" (along with "accentuation" and "fixation") as one of the adaptive processes which operate in perception itself. More recently, L. Postman has offered experimental evidence for the "mechanisms" which determine perceptual selection. Briefly, "selection" as a value-orientation, becomes a determinant of what is perceived and noted by functioning as: a) a sensitizer (lowering thresholds for acceptable stimuli); b) as a repressor (raising thresholds for unacceptable stimuli) and c) as a generalizer (whatever the nature of the stimulus, it makes for ready perception of stimuli which lie within the same value-area as is already preferred.) In Postman's words: "The experimental evidence leads us to the formulation of three mechanisms ... Value-orientation makes for perceptual sensitization to valued stimuli, leads to perceptual defense against inimical stimuli, and gives rise to a process of value-resonance which keeps the person responding in terms of objects valued by him even when such objects are absent from his immediate environment. These processes of selection must be considered in any perceptual theory which lays claim to comprehensiveness" [17].

Illustrations such as this, as well as so many others in other contexts, suggest that Cassirer has touched off a more productive response on the part of many scientists, whom he did not overtly address, than of philosophers who, for the most part, still talk of perception and language in terms which make them contemporaries of faculty- and associationist psychologists as of old.

Where positivistically oriented semioticians have restricted their analyses to the actual body of sentences permissible within constructed sample languages or samples of actual languages, Cassirer's interests range from the complex languages of myth to the highly constructive languages of mathematics and physics, with the purpose of indicating for them all their characteristic "foci of attention", their perspectives of noting which, in turn, determine their respective types of "denotation" and "designation".

All of the above really amounts to the assertion that, in studying forms of signification, we always presuppose signs, not only in the sense of a meta-language in which to talk about them, but also in the sense that, whatever it is to which signs are assigned, it must already participate in some sign-context to have any meaning at all or, at any rate, to have a meaning sufficiently determinate to make possible the attachment to it of one, rather than any other, linguistic sign. Positivists, whose interests are at once highly formal and emphatically practical (if not outright therapeutical) have aimed primarily at rendering language as unambiguous a medium of communication as possible. Consequently, they have focussed on the problem of designation as it arises on the "semantical" level of conventional sign-systems where decisions with respect to correct usage can best be made. Once sign-usages are fixed, precise reference becomes possible. In contrast, Cassirer has approached language not in order to leave it a more satisfactory means of communication, but in order to understand it as the cultural medium par excellence through which man both organizes and articulates his world.

To the extent that this "organization and articulation" is of a consciously-constructive kind, Cassirer, in his studies of modern mathematical physics, has examined its conventional language-systems in a manner only terminologically dissimilar from the positivistic analyses. In their reviews of his *Substance and Function* [18] and *Determinismus and Indeterminismus in der modernen Physik* [19], both H. Reichenbach and Ph. Franck have come to an essentially favorable estimate of Cassirer's "philosophy of science".

It is, however, one of Cassirer's principal tenets that comparatively consistent contexts of signification also occur, and have to be accounted for, in the case of the metaphorical languages of myth, commonsense or art. His frequent assertion that a "naming activity" precedes all consciously effected concept-formation, that we must study the multiple directions of "noting" in order to understand the "properties" and "objects" which become the "denotata" of a more conscious sign-use, all this leads to Cassirer's insistence that philosophers should pay as much attention to the level of primary sign-*production* as they have already given to the scientific levels of sign-*assignment*.

This enlargement of the philosopher's concern for sign-situations beyond the domains where they have conventionally been looked for, must bring up a problem of method. How can rational discourse, how can philosophy, which historically came into its own by having broken away from the 'confusion' of myth, presume to discover an organization, a "cosmos" in what it left behind a mere "chaos" of "non-being?" The best answer to this question is, of course, to be looked for in Cassirer's actual investigations of the languages of myth and commonsense as they are given in the first two volumes of the *Philosophie der Symbolischen Formen*.

What is of methodological importance in this connection can perhaps be summarized in this fashion:

1) Philosophy, in establishing early in its career the ideal of a "rational" (demonstrative) language and, after the advent of science, giving preferential consideration especially to the mathematical and mechanical symbol-systems, has lost sight of the more complex and less precise, yet still appreciably ordered "languages" of commonsense, myth and art which would satisfy

the requirement of being "languages" in that they establish (though less consciously and more ambiguously) relations between their signs, and thus their own "vocabularies" and "grammars". If we define languages as conventional sign-systems and if, in turn, we call "conventional" only those systems in which designation arises as a result of considered decisions, then, of course, there can be no semantics to the metaphorical languages whose primary and pervasive character is so strongly emphasized by Cassirer. If, on the other hand, we look upon every sign-context as "conventional", (even if its users accept it as a "gift" from the gods, and thus as non-conventional in the sense of being in harmony with the "nature of things") by reason of its dependency upon human "perspectives" or teleological "foci of sight", then, just as clearly, there will occur semantical issues on levels of signification barely noticed by philosophers so far.

2) What interest is the philosopher to take in those proposed studies of the ways in which signs can make sense on the mythical and metaphorical levels? To Cassirer, as we have seen, the understanding of "pre-scientific" symbolisms is not of primarily historical import. When examining the rich cargo of source-material unearthed by him, Cassirer is clearly not concerned with the respective "worlds" of the Kwakiutl, Sioux or the Melanesians per se. Instead, such studies of primitive as well as civilized ritual and verbal symbolisms are offered as evidence for the thesis that there are (or have been) structured "universes of discourse" corresponding to differently centered "universes of action". To speak here of "universes" would merely mean that, prior to the working out of rationally constructed systems, we are to account for (because we are faced with) experiences as structured and reflected by ritualistic and linguistic systems, for which philosophical reflection should indicate their respective "frames of reference". By a "frame of reference", we mean, in this connection, that just as all assertions made in rational discourse are, in principle, grounded in a set of syntactic and semantic rules, so there is also, for pre-scientific sign-contexts, a pervasive, though variously modifiable, reference to such basic "principles of division" as, e.g., the "Holy" and the "Profane", the "Light" and the "Dark", the archetypal organization of the human body, etc. There is, in other words, some "thought" (sense) involved in both

scientific and mythical world-experiencing. In one instance, to be sure, thought is controlled by specifiable assumptions and demonstrable derivations, in the other it is "oriented", with less sensitivity to contradiction, around more or less clearly articulated "foci of attention", grounded in "feeling-tones" (on the emotive-expressive dimension) or preferences of volition and action (on the intuitional-commonsense dimension).

Cassirer's "foci of attention" or "feeling tones", his "preferences of volition and action" are, to be sure, the equivalents of "norms", "value-orientation" "need- and gratification" concepts of contemporary social science terminology. While the anthropological case for a variety of culturally possible world-interpretations is commonly shared by now, we are still far from well-documented and concise explorations of the connections between these cultural variations and their dependency upon the rigidifying function of linguistic pre-direction on the one hand, and between grammars and fashions of speaking in their connection with selective value-patterns on the other. Benjamin Lee Whorf, commenting upon his comparative study of Indogermanic and Hopi speech-patterns, points in the direction of more specific work to be done. If the Hopi can neither speak nor think about their world in the space-time-and matter categories which appear so "natural" to most Western cultures; if, on the other hand, Western speech-and thought habits can easily take to a Euclidean and Newtonian "unit"-universe (but find it difficult to imagine the energy- and event universe postulated by modern physics), then we ought to be able to account for such approach-differences in terms of the actual and practical concerns which distinguish Western action-patterns from those of the Hopi. "The need for measurement in industry and trade, the stores and bulks of "stuff" in various containers, the type-bodies in which various goods were handled, standardized measure and weight units, invention of clocks and measurement of "time", keeping records, accounts, chronicles, histories, mathematics ... all cooperated to bring our thought and language world into its present form" [20].

As we shall have more acute and better documented analyses of the relationships between language, thought and common action-patterns of groups, it will also become possible to work out "pragmatics" for differently oriented languages of myth and commonsense. We would have to infer from them the directions of interest, the teleological perspectives which govern what is noted and seen as well as what must remain unseen and unnoticed by them. "Whatever appears important for our wishing and willing, our hope and anxiety, for acting and doing: that and only that receives the stamp of verbal meaning ... Only what is related somehow to the focus point of willing and doing, only what proves to be essential to the whole scheme of life and acti-vity is selected ... and noticed ... (Such) distinctions in meaning are the prerequisite for that solidification of impressions which .. is a necessary condition for their denotation by words" [21].

To let one illustration stand for many: if, for purposes of communication, we derive from empirical observation of specific behavior that, what we call "moon", is called "luna" by other sign-users, we know all we need to understand (or be understood by them) on occasions where the word-symbol "luna" occurs. If, on the other hand, we want to understand language in its "objectifying" role, what we would care to know is why, what we call "moon", is noticed and denoted differently as the "luminous one" (in Latin) or the "measuring one" (in Greek). Why, in other words, are the selfsame optical data "seen" as signs of quite differently experienced objects? To answer a question of this type, we would have to refer signs not only to overtly observable behavior connected with their use but also to other signs of already established meaning. To speak of the "objectifying" office of signs, besides their indicative or communicative roles, is not synony-mous with the demand that an empirical reading of sign-behav-ior should be replaced by the more "profound" evidences of an introspective interpretation. It would be required, however, that the empirically established designations are, in turn, subjected to an interpretation whose aim it would be to "reconstruct" the pragmatic attitudes and "centers of attention" from the "voca-bulary" through which they articulate their respective angles of vision. If, for the purpose of such an interpretation, we examine similarities or shifts of meaning as they hold among signs, either within a language or between languages, we will, of course, not be investigating such relations between signs as the syntactical branch of semiotics is charged with formalizing. Employing comparative methods, we would rather be inferring from (actual or recorded) ritualistic or verbal sign-usages the pervasive "perspectives" which determine the selection of what is both noted and denoted.

3) Granted an interest in the type of inquiry just mentioned, what importance would it have as compared to the semiotician's concern with language-analysis? According to Cassirer, this "apparent overstepping of the usual boundaries of logical inquiry" will do two things for us: it will make us understand more clearly the structure of our perceptually-experienced world from which all rational thought must depart if it is to perform its distinctive task. This point is programmatically put by Usener, a mythologist and philologist much admired and often quoted by Cassirer: "Our epistemology will not have any real foundation until the sciences of language and mythology have revealed the processes of involuntary and unconscious modes of representation. The chasm between specific perceptions and general concepts is far greater than our academic notions and a language which does our thinking for us lead us to suppose. It is so great that I cannot imagine how it could have been bridged, had not language itself, without man's conscious awareness, prepared and induced the process. It is language that causes the multitude of casual, individual expressions to yield up one which extends its denotation over more and more special cases, until it comes to denote them all, and assumes the power of expressing a class-concept" [22].

Cassirer's own studies on language and myth in his books, monographs and such essays as, e.g., his *Language and the Construction of the Object-world* [23] constitute so many attempts to sketch the outline of an answer to Usener's challenge. This challenge, in brief, is to disclose language not only as the verbal "formulater" but also as the active "agency" through which a manifold of impressions is broken into the "things" and "persons" of perceptual experience. How can language be disclosed as such an agency? We have in an earlier chapter indicated some of the mythological and linguistic evidence for this contention.

Empirical evidence has multiplied far beyond the state at which Cassirer undertook his pioneering generalizations. Among sociologists, e.g., C. W. Mills registers recognition that language operates socially not just as a means if communication, but that it molds and perpetuates social perception. "Language, socially built and maintained, embodies implicit exhortations and social evaluations. By acquiring the catagories of language, we acquire the structured "ways" of a group, and along with the language, the value-implicates of those 'ways' ... A vocabulary is not merely a string of words, immanent within it are social textures, institutional and political coordinates. Back of a vocabulary lie sets of political action" [24].

Among physiologists, Kurt Goldstein ammassed impressive evidence from aphasia-patients whose perception- and action capacities co-varied with damage to brain-areas which control (abstract) speech. Goldstein draws from them the conclusion that "the function of naming objects does not represent a simple superficial connection between a thing and a word. We know that language is more than a mere reflection of outside objects in the mind, that it is rather a means itself for building up the world in a particular way" [25].

Among linguists, Benjamin Lee Whorf has even spoken of a "linguistic principle of relativity" which, in informal terms, means" that users of markedly different grammars are pointed .. toward different types of observation and different evaluations of externally similar acts of observation" [26]. Generalizing upon years of study of the Hopi-language, Whorf (without ever indicating that he read Cassirer) comes to conclusions which could have come from Cassirer himself: "It was found that the background linguistic system ... of each language is not merely a reproducing instrument for voicing ideas, but rather is itself the shaper of ideas, the program and guide for the individual's mental activity, for his analysis of impressions, for his synthesis of his mental stock in trade ... The categories and types that we isolate from the world of phenomena we do not find there because they stare every observer in the face; on the contrary, the world is presented in a kaleidoscopic flux of impressions which has to be organized by our minds – and this means largely by the linguistic systems ... We cut nature up, organize it into concepts, and ascribe significances as we do largely because we are parties to an agreement to organize it this way – an agreement that holds throughout our speech community and is codified in the patterns of our language ... We are thus introduced to a new principle of relativity which holds that all observers are not led by the same physical evidence to the same picture of the universe, unless their linguistic backgrounds are similar or can be calibrated" [27].

Among child-psychologists, Cassirer had been impressed by the work of Piaget and Buehler who called his attention to the circumstance that the diffuse perceptual discriminations of the young child went hand in hand with its equally diffuse verbal responses. The "names" it uses at first do not designate any clearly distinguished objects or persons at all; instead they appear to accompany certain vague and fluctuating complex impressions. "The mother has to put on a different hat ... a thing just has to change position within the room to appear "strange" to the child in whom they will not touch off the otherwise regularly produced word" [28]. The interpretation which, according to Cassirer, we must put upon this (as well as so many other illustrations from child, animal, primitive- and abnormal psychology) is as follows: it is only to the extent that the name-words break through an initial phase of attachment to complex impressions in order to become applied, in a more universal fashion, to a variety of aspects that the child will eventually come to experience its world as consisting of things and persons. Quite typically, the child does not ask "what is the name of this thing"? but rather: "what is it?" "What" the thing is, and "how it is called", are both fused into one; the child "has" the object in and by means of the name. Verbal signs, we must conclude, are involved in "arresting" certain perceptual units long before they can be formally "assigned" to them as their "names" for purposes of communication. "Only when the meaning of the word is acquired can "being" itself come to a halt for our (mental) sight". (Jetzt erst, nachdem der Sinn des Namens gewonnen ist, hält auch das Sein dem Blicke stand) [29].

There is a further advantage in this realization of the "constructive" role of language: it opens up a clearer conception of exactly what the rational discourse of the sciences can and cannot do. Ever since Plato aimed to "save the appearances" by having them participate in the reality of the "ideas", the hiatus between the realm of perception on one hand and the constructive (mostly mathematical and mechanical) symbolisms of conceptual knowledge on the other, has been the "pièce de résistance" for many philosophical systems. Theories of knowledge, oriented toward the cognitive ideal of science, could at best hope either to discredit the mere "having" of perceptions or to isolate those factors, ("conditions") which our "minds" supposedly had to bring into play in order to bring forth reliable (i. e., scientific) knowledge. One could say, perhaps, that most, if not all, epistemologies have remained somewhat unplausible because of the circumstance that the type of knowledge "explained" by them (in terms of ideas, associations, categories, etc.) never seemed to throw much light upon that world in which man actually lives and operates. Between the "given-ness" of sense-data and perceptions on one side and the type of objectivity posited by the exact sciences, the "actual world" remained unaccounted for – and this in spite of the fact that it clearly exhibited some order and structure, however inexact, of its own. More recently, writers in epistemology have accordingly preferred to start from what has been called the "concreta"-basis, the world of things as we see them, at once more than a mere flux of impressions and yet not possessing the coherence required of knowledge that could issue in science. "The basis of epistemological construction therefore is the world of concrete objects; from this sphere, inferences lead to more complex physical objects on the one hand, and to impressions on the other" [30]. Now, it is this "concreta"-basis, either neglected or taken for granted, which would become illuminated in a language-analysis of the type advocated by Cassirer. If, as he points out, we experience our world (pre-scientifically) essentially as language "divides" and orders it for us, and if, furthermore, these "divisions" can be comprehended in terms of differently focussed perspectives of feeling or action, then, it would seem, the "concreta"-basis, taken as a "terminus a quo" for other epistemologies, would become a "terminus ad quem" for a philosophy of symbolic forms which proposes to examine impartially all meaningful contexts of experience as so many types of sign-functioning on different levels of representation.

The perception of concrete objects and persons, while "given" and "immediate", pre-analytically considered, turns out, upon reflection, to be itself the outcome of what Cassirer calls a "symbolic" breakthrough, a "naming madness" (Manie der Benennung) which signalizes "an intellectual revolution ... (if one) has learned to use words not merely as mechanical signs or signals but as an entirely new instrument of thought ... a new horizon is opened up. The principle of symbolism, with its universality, validity and general applicability is the magic word, the Open Sesame, giving access to the specifically human world, to the world of human culture. Once man is in possession of this magic key, further progress is assured" [31].

THE PRAGMATIC DIMENSION OF SIGN-FUNCTIONING

We have, in the preceding section, distinguished the semiotician's concern with the "indicative" or "informative" sign-usages and their relevance for overt behavior from Cassirer's interest in what he calls the "objectifying", i.e., "symbolic" sign-function. While apparently true to the letter of the pronouncements of these two schools of thought, this formulation requires some further qualification. Such general names as "perspectives", "organs" of reality, etc., are, after all, but metaphorical ways of referring to modes of activity. In this manner Cassirer himself has read what he considered Kant's "transcendental revolution". For this reason alone, it cannot be illuminating simply to op-pose Cassirer's "idealistic" interpretation to a "scientifically behavioristic" one. Cassirer's insistence on "the primacy of the function" (das Primat der Funktion vor dem Gegenstand), as well as the semiotician's conviction that "pragmatic observations are the basis of all linguistic research" [32], can both be looked at as variants of a sign-interpretation oriented toward the same primary datum: activities. If so considered, Cassirer's philosophy of symbolic forms would provide us with a less neatly classified, though more circumspect, framework of inquiry into the cultur-ally possible "contexts of meaning", an inquiry, furthermore, for which both the semantical and pragmatical levels of sign-analysis would have to be considerably enlarged. So far, we have briefly sketched the extension required with respect to the semantical issue of designation. We must now give some attention to the type of pragmatics implied in Cassirer's theory of symbolic forms.

Cassirer's invitation to study the different modalities of sym-bolic sign-functioning, (as manifest in the various mythological, religious, artistic, practical or scientific forms of experiencing), clearly implies the proposal to extend the domain of pragmatics beyond "an empirical discipline dealing with a special kind of behavior" [33]. Account must be taken also of those "activities" which, though not overtly observable, can be inferred in a "re-constructive" interpretation. If pragmatic analysis is extended beyond the comparatively "poor" languages, formalized by Carnap, e.g., to also include the language of physics, one is usually quite aware that an understanding of the procedure involved can hardly be read from empirical observations of the physicist's overt doings alone. What one must do, instead, is "to construct thinking processes in a way in which they ought to occur if they are to be ranged in a consistent system; or to construct justifiable sets of operations which can be intercalated between the starting point and the issue of thought processes, replacing the real inter-mediary links" [31]. For a formalization of a "pragmatics" of physical language, it would therefore not be sufficient to confine oneself to the empirically observable acts by which the physicist "proceeds" as a matter of fact; we would have to formalize his "procedure" which must be inferred in a "rational reconstruction." The explanatory value of such reconstruction would concern not so much physics, taken as a "corpus" of propositions accepted at a given time, but the language of physics, defined in terms of rules of procedure. It has been said, accordingly, that "symbols in physics do indeed stand for operations – but we have to let a symbol stand for a concept which is, so to speak, the synthesis of the results of a whole set of operations which may appear to be superficially dissimilar (in the "context of observation;") but are assumed by the physicist to have a common element (in the "context of reconstruction") [35].

A more generously conceived discipline of "pragmatics" would therefore have to be concerned not only with the biological, psychological or sociological inquiries in connection with the fact of the acceptance of "procedures", but also with the problem of the justification of such acceptance. This distinction has been re-cognized by Reichenbach as germane to two different contexts: the context of discovery and the context of justification [36]. With-in the former, we are concerned with such actual processes as have proven instrumental in the evolution of what Dewey calls "successful habits of inquiry" [37]. In the admittedly less empirical context of justification, we aim at the formulation of what have been called "preference rules" which, indirectly and via "basic rules of procedure", govern the structure of science with their prescriptions for: unity, simplicity, unrestricted universality, precision and pervasiveness of law [38].

To recognize that one is doing "pragmatics" in either case is not to level the difference between these two distinct inquiries. Whether we investigate empirically the active behavior of the scientist or whether we inferentially reconstruct his procedure which defines those acts that are "justifiable" for him, we are in each case attempting to explain an (empirical or procedural) order-context, with reference to activities, selectivities and preferences. Moreover: observation of the "proceedings" of the scientist presupposes familiarity with the procedurally permissible steps of deduction and confirmation; otherwise there is no telling which of the "observed acts" are done by the scientist "qua scientist" and not "qua erring human being". The meta-linguistic, pragmatic rules which can be formulated with respect to scientific procedure are not empirical in the sense in which, guided by these procedures, scientific rules themselves are empirical, if not analytic. A "pragmatics" for the conventional symbolic sign-systems of the sciences can thus not be given in terms of empirical descriptions alone; it involves an inferential reconstruction of "aims" and "preferences" from the actual structure of these systems.

While a detailed account of the character of such reconstructions is not to the point here, two somewhat different types of reconstruction should be noted: *a*) a "logical reconstruction" for both the basic and the specifically methodological rules of the various sciences, and *b*) a "comparative reconstruction" for the "preference rules", the "regulative ideals" of any and all inquiries claiming to be "scientific". Outstanding examples of the first kind have been given us by Whitehead, Russell, the positivists and Cassirer himself; for an illustration of the "comparative" interpretation we mention Dewey's well-formulated contrast-interpretations of the scientific (as distinguished from common-sense or esthetic) meaning-contexts.

What type of "reconstruction" is employed by Cassirer for the purpose of arriving at a "pragmatics" in which full and impartial attention can be given to all the various "perspectives" and "preference rules" which, implicitly or explicitly, determine the modes in which human minds can interpret (sensory) signs as making "sense?" To ask this question is synonymous with asking for the meaning of such words as "analysis", "interpretation", etc., which we have used to designate Cassirer's "inquiry" into symbolic forms. What sort of "analysis" are we actually offered? Is there evidence on the strength of which we must accept his findings? If so, then what is this evidence? Answers to these questions can unfortunately not easily be given in terms of definite references to the text. Cassirer still writes manifestly in the grand style of German idealism. And this means two things: he writes such appealing and forceful cadences as can only be appreciated by one not yet familiar with – or already on the rebound from – the terse prose of positivism; it also means that many of his arguments and interpretations are expressed in metaphorical language, lacking in that methodological self-consciousness that has improved some, and frustrated more, of contemporary writings in philosophy. As a result, we are faced with the somewhat paradoxical situation that a thinker who has investigated many, including primitive and abnormal symbolisms, scarcely makes his own language and procedure a topic of investigation. To say this, however, is no admission that one could not infer his method from his work. If we examine the inquiries Cassirer actually undertakes of the various modes of symbolic functioning in his books on myth, language, perceptual and conceptual knowledge, what do we find him doing? We are given, on one hand, ever new presentations of his general thesis, on the other, an impressive wealth of factual data, drawn from the entire conspectus of human culture which, if the thesis be accepted, would indeed constitute a richer amount and diversity of evidence than is ordinarily found in philosophical works. The question remains: by reason of which considerations is the thesis to be accepted?

Our exposition of the meaning of the thesis could perhaps be summarized here: philosophy must aim to understand all culturally given types of experience-accounting in terms of symbolic sign-functions; it furthermore must indicate for every one of these functions their specific directions of synthetizing the sensory manifold with reference to the dominant foci of feeling, willing and thinking. If this be the meaning of Cassirer's thesis, how can it be ascertained in the face of the positivist's strictures to the effect that all meaningful discourse can either be empirically- descriptive or analytically-tautologous?

Clearly, Cassirer's reference to "human foci of feeling, willing and thinking", while related to a wealth of empirical data, is just as manifestly not offered as a description of dated events. Surely, one must have already decided on what one will understand by a "dominant focus", on sign-functions as determining meaning-contexts, before one can proceed to describe what are taken as empirical instances of this conviction. Is the rationale of Cassirer's thesis then of an analytic type? If by an analytic statement be understood a formula the truth of which is independent of the truth-values of the elementary propositions which make it up (Wittgenstein), or as a statement not designating things but significant only with respect to the syntax of language (Carnap), then Cassirer's thesis would be meaningless on both counts. It is presented neither as an empirical description, nor can it simply be regarded as a formula concerning the use and "transformability" of sets of linguistic signs.

Strictly positivist semioticians would accordingly have to invoke against Cassirer's whole enterprise Wittgenstein's famous dictum that "whereof one *cannot* speak, thereof one *must* be silent" [39]. It can be shown, however, that this article of philosophical sobriety, if interpreted as analytic of all assertions, cannot be offered as a maxim for avoiding some assertions; if interpreted as analytic for some, namely descriptive assertions, it is invalid for all assertions; and if interpreted as a prescription, it cannot be grounded within the positivist frame of reference.

Interpretation of this injunctive maxim will hinge on the meanings assigned to both "cannot" and "must". Which criteria are to determine what "can" and what "cannot" be said, not in this or that, but in any language? If the criteria are of a syntactical type, involving the laws of logic, then "whereof one cannot speak" refers to the logical impossibility, not of expressing beliefs and feelings, but of communicating them by way of words and sentences which violate the principles of logically consistent discourse. The apparently exhortative "thereof one *must* be silent" takes a correspondingly logical meaning, and thus the dictum amounts to the statement that "whatever cannot be asserted without contradiction cannot be asserted as communication". Such a statement would be meaningful only at the price of being pointless as a recommendation. What must be the case in a logical sense, cannot fail to be the case in a sense open to correction by this, or any other, maxim of language-use. To be sure, one can fail to be logical, and to that extent one will fail to communicate effectively. But interpreted analytically, the maxim merely expresses the conditional that if one cannot use language in conformity to criteria of consistency, then one cannot expect to make logical sense. It does not, however, legislate that we cannot use language in any other way.

If "whereof one cannot speak" refers to the semantical impossibility of either having words or of so using them that they clearly designate some state of affairs, then the implication that "one must be silent" is either tautologous or false. It is tautologous, since the lack of direct or indirect linguistic expressions is synonymous with "being silent"; it is false, since the lack of clearly designative expressions has never yet prevented individuals from using language for other than designative purposes.

What the proponents of the dictum may want to assert is likely to be something else. They may have in mind to formulate a stricture with regard to any language-use that fails to be formally or factually communicative. "Whereof one cannot speak" in conformity with syntactical and semantical rules which govern consistent and designative language-use, "thereof" one had better not speak at all. This injunction, however, not to realize through language purposes other than those furthered by interpersonally reliable communication is entailed neither as a "must" by the meaning of language nor, indeed, by factually true propositions about the linguistic behavior of men.

It would appear, therefore, that the dictum not to resort to language where it cannot serve the purposes of communicative discourse must be interpreted as a prescription for, rather than as a description or analysis of, language-use. If so interpreted, it means more than the tautology that language, to become communication, must abide by formal and designative rules which define language as communication. Rather does it imply the non-logical prescription that language, if not used for communication, should not be used at all. This maxim is demonstrable only if, besides the premise that "only designative language can contain true or false propositions", another premise is added to the effect that "only true or false propositions are worth making". This second premise, however, is neither implied in the meaning of language nor empirically derived from the observation of actual language-behavior. Instead, it formulates a preference for the outcome of the linguistic behavior of those who do use language in a certain, i.e., communicative way. Thus, a value-commitment is implied; only communicative discourse is worth making. Unfortunately, on the positivist program, preferences for the realization of some rather than of other values, enjoy no cognitive status whatever. The admonition not to use language except as an instrument of communication is tantamount to expressing a value-judgment in favor of cognitively relevant propositions. But value-expressions, in the positivist account, are not assertible in propositional form at all. They occur, grammatically camouflaged as propositions, in linguistic expressions of wishes and attitudes. Therefore, to utter "Either use language to make logically consistent and factually designative sense or don't use it at all" can only be offered as a "proposal" which, not testable as either true or false, manifests a non-factual linguistic expression of preference for the value of communicative language or for such values as may be realized by its employment.

We conclude that the prescriptive maxim under consideration is not itself an example of the type of language-use which it prescribes. This self-liquidating consequence can be avoided only if value expressions also are accomodated within the privileged class of those cognitively respectable propositions "whereof one can speak". If so certified, the meaning-requirements which constitute the positivist program would have to be greatly modified. If not, the injunction that "whereof one cannot speak, thereof one must be silent" can itself not be stated as a maxim prescriptive for anybody but its proponents ... who must remain silent. If so, there really is no argument at all.

We have already noted (see p. 78) that when Cassirer had to defend himself against the charge of logical inconsistency regarding the symbol-concept, he preferred to counter such objections by showing that, if entertained, they would invalidate not only his particular theory of symbolic forms, but all of mathematical science as well. Why doubt, he says in effect, on logical grounds what, as a matter of fact, exists and works? [40]. In a variation to this approach to objections, one could perhaps meet the, as yet unvoiced, positivistic strictures against a philosophy which is neither strictly descriptive nor strictly analytic, by pointing out that, on the same count, neither certain scientific laws nor the program of positivism could be meaningfully asserted. Take the physical "law of inertia": it neither describes actual states of affairs nor does it simply formulate a decision with regard to linguistic usage. And the program of positivism: can its disjunctive thesis that "all valid (or true) statements are either analytically syntactical or empirically descriptive" be grounded by either tautologies or descriptions? Now, positivists, when confronted with this question, will presumably point out that this disjunction is to be taken in a hypothetical mood which, in this case, would mean that the validity of their decision about meaningful statements would, in turn, have to be legitimized in terms of the ultimate (and non-hypothetical) criterion for all empirically meaningful statements: i.e. verification (resp. confirmation). The validity of this criterion, however, cannot again be grounded either analytically or by empirical verification. So, unless we are to get into an infinite regress of verifying that and what we are verifying, a decision must be reached sometime, resulting in statements to the effect that (unless analytically derivable) all meaningful statements "should" be verifiable. The character of such a statement of the thesis is certainly not descriptive, but rather prescriptive with respect to the way in which meaningful statements are to be constructed and tested.

Two further thoughts are relevant in this connection: the decision as to which kind of statement "should" be taken as "valid" or "true" in syntactical or semantical contexts obviously arises from a considered examination of actual validity- (truth-) claiming statements – and also a preference for some of them. It arises, we suggest, from a comparative interpretation of a type essentially similar in character to the inferential pragmatic reconstructions employed both by the philosopher of science (Reichenbach,

Kaufman, Margenau, etc.) and in Cassirer's actual argument for a philosophy of symbolic form. The positivist's examination of the various "truth-candidates" among assertions, his preference for one or two of them, constitutes itself a decision which could be formulated as a high-level generalization of the sort: "statements susceptible to verification by statements about matters of fact are more reliable (as a matter of fact and with regard to facts) than statements not so reducible". A generalization of this kind – not itself descriptive but about descriptions – is raised to the level of an "analytic truth" by simply considering it as definitory of all (empirically) meaningful statements. The logical character of such a definition, we suggest, is of the same "prescriptive" and "regulative" kind as has been conceded for the status of such physical "laws" as, e.g., the "law of inertia" which can be taken as "defining (jointly with the second law of motion from which it is deducible as the special case $F = 0$) a method of describing motion" [41].

Neither the sort of considerations, it seems, by reason of which the positivist's program has been proposed, nor those by virtue of which empirical generalizations have been raised to the status of laws, nor finally, those that traditionally have been of import in the philosophical enterprise, can be accounted for in terms of the Scylla of being "empirically descriptive" or the Charybdis of "constituting issues of language". Instead, both the assertions which formulate the grounds of the positivist's program and the formulations which ground the meaning of physical laws are plausibly interpreted as empirical generalizations, hypothetically suggested, which, on the strength of the accumulating evidence for them, can become "conditions for the possibility" of the range of phenomena to which they apply; be it in terms of regulative prescriptions, be it in terms of a coherent framework of explanation. Cassirer's own thesis that all empirical meaning-contexts (structures) are best interpreted as so many manifestations of "sense in the senses", as differently centered modes of symbolic representation by means of sensory cues, is neither deductively reached by specifiable steps from an antecedent "axiomatic", nor is it presented as an empirical description of how, in space and time, human beings have, as a matter or fact, built up their cultural worlds by, consciously or not, employing "symbolic forms". As an empirical generalization on the highest possible level of generalization, the thesis is confronted, however, with such a diversity of material drawn from the "natural" and "cultural" sciences that, to the extent as it turns out to be comprehensively applicable to them, it is finally commended as being "definitory" of all phenomena considered.

How, at this point, Cassirer's theory of symbolic forms makes contact with Kant's "transcendental method" is notable. Kant's merit – in Cassirer's interpretation (see p. 50) – was to have discouraged the philosopher's concern with "being qua being" and to have turned it, instead, toward an inquiry that would isolate – in a "Kritik" – those principles and categories which can be recognized as being "constitutive" of experience (as science).Kant's error was not to have considered alternatives to these "ordering principles" and thus to have "frozen" them into immutable faculties. The philosophy of symbolic forms is Kantian in spirit only insofar as it, too, declares it to be the task of philosophy to formulate the most universal functions of organization and synthetizing for all types of human experience. Neither Kant nor Cassirer depart from the evidences of "introspection" or the sense-data basis; both start with experience as publicly accessible, be it the factuality of science or that of myth, religion, art and the perceptual world of commonsense. So far their agreement. In contradistinction from Kant, Cassirer has not sought for an "anchoring ground" of the various symbolic "perspectives" which condition all culturally encountered "orders" in any intrinsic constitution of the human "mind". Only "pragmatic" considerations can account for the special directions of "sight" which organize (serialize) the sensory impressions into representative contexts of meaning. Thus, Cassirer speaks of the "teleological structure of our commonsense world" as it is reflected in our "language-concepts" [42]. In one of his last books, he remarks: "Between our practical and theoretical concepts there is no basic difference insofar as all our theoretical concepts share the character of instrumentality. They, too, are – in a final analysis – but tools which we have to create for the solution of specific tasks and which we have ever to recreate" [43].

In the light of this pragmatic outlook, Cassirer's symbolic-form concept itself must be viewed as an "instrument" serving the philosophical "interest" of reaching a concept so universal that it can define all cultural "domains of objectivity" as so many modally distinct sign-systems which, themselves, are "instrumental" to the various "foci of interest", the "centers of attention", all of which look from different angles and for different purposes at the selfsame "manifold of sense impressions".

Clearly, no final verification of such a general proposition is possible. It is open to confirmation, however, by the disciplines which determine "what the facts are" in their respective domains of inquiry. In this sense, Cassirer has expressed the hope that this philosophy may achieve for the humanities (Geisteswissenschaften) what Kant had first attempted for Newtonian physics [44]. To be sure, if it can be shown that in the several domains of physics, psychology, linguistics, mythology, etc., their characteristic objects of inquiry are not chips from the old block "reality", but that they are plausibly interpreted as perceptions signifying differently in different modes of symbolic representation, if this can be shown to be so, then a philosophy which could indicate for all of these domains their specific type of sign-functioning would indeed deserve the importance with which Cassirer regards it. The question remains whether this can be shown as a matter of fact. Cassirer himself thought that, ever since the last century, authoritative representatives of many fields of inquiry have actually come to realize the symbolical nature of their subject-matters [45]. These are the "big five" to whom Cassirer refers most frequently: Hilbert (for Logic), Herz (for Physics), Helmholtz (for Psycho-physiology), Humboldt (for Linguistics) and Herder (for Poetry). Many other names could be – and have been – suggested [46]. One's decision as to whether all these investigations do or do not support Cassirer's interpretation will, of course, depend upon both one's own understanding of the evidence and the degree to which further development in the "natural" and "cultural" disciplines will clinch the case for the philosophy of "symbolic forms".

CHAPTER VII

THE SEMIOTIC RANGE OF PHILOSOPHY

Recent logical, epistemological and value-theoretical contributions to the general field of philosophy seem to confirm the impression that for all of them the ultimate referents of any symbolic or meaning context (of rules, laws or norms) are always those "units of reality" which, traditionally, have been called "particulars" and, more recently, "events". However otherwise classified, events appear to enter into either one or all three of the following contexts:

(1) a formal sign-context: as the physical vehicles of symbols in language;

(2) an empirical sign-context: as the referents of what a language names, i.e. the non-conventional events, designated by the events which are the vehicles of the conventional language-symbols;

(3) a pragmatic sign-context: as the referents of value-statements; i.e., of such properties of (either conventional or unconventional) events as have bearing upon human concerns.

It would appear, therefore, that "events" enter into the cultural polyphony of all meaning-melodies in the various keys of validity, truth and value. Philosophical problems, however diversified, could then be said to be dominated by the leit-motifs of the perennial themes of rational consistency, empirical reliability and human goodness. This formulation is sufficiently close to the positivist conception of philosophy as semiotics to suggest their tri-partite division of philosophical analysis into the sign-dimensions of syntax, semantics and pragmatics. This classification, it will be recalled, follows from their definition of a sign-situation as involving the three variables of sign-event, signified event and sign-interpretant, and from isolating either the conventional relations between signs, the conventional relations between sign and signified events and the empirical relation between sign-interpretant and his sign-selections.

Perhaps the most obvious comment upon this scheme should be the observation that it exhausts the scope neither of all non-discursive types of signification, elicited by Cassirer, nor of the discursive sign-contexts nor, by implication, of those signcontexts in which all genuine philosophical work can be carried on. Thus, not all necessary relations may turn out to be merely conventional, not all significantly designative discourse need be either in or about the language of science, and human purposes may be sensitive to cognitive direction in ways not covered by empirical "pragmatics".

Yet, and from this assumption I shall proceed, there is a perfectly good sense in which one can say that philosophical inquiries are after all so many interpretations of events with respect to 1) their mutual consistency, 2) their empirical [expressive or designative] meaning or 3) their meaning for the "good life". In this chapter I shall not argue for this scheme by indicating how its quite simple classification, which threatens to swallow all significant detail, nevertheless provides a terminological key into which the entire philosophical tradition can be translated. Nor will I discuss the advantages which may be gained from its adoption. On this score, the positivist claims have been rather articulate. Instead, I shall confine myself to the preparatory task of examining some of the shortcomings of their orientation which, I believe, have obscured the potential merit of viewing the cognitive quest in the semiotic media of formal, factual or valuational sign-contexts.

In what follows I hope to make plausible the contention that actual and possible objections to our semiotic scheme do not touch the comprehensiveness of its basic divisions into formal, designative and valuational discourse, but that they attach rather to some of its currently influential interpretations. I turn therefore to a defense of this scheme against what I consider unduly narrow conceptions of its positivistically informed proponents. In support of my belief that semiotics allows for a wider range of philosophical work than can be certified by linguistically preoccupied thinkers, I propose to comment on five propositions which I take to be programmatic of their interpretation of the basic sign-processes. As my point of departure I select a passage from Reichenbach's *The Rise Of Scientific Philosophy*: "One conclusion can immediately be drawn from an analysis of modern science —— Knowledge divides into synthetic and analytic statements; the synthetic statements inform us about matters of fact; the analytic statements are empty ... The modern analysis of knowledge makes a cognitive ethics impossible".

The above three sentences contain four propositions and presuppose a fifth one, namely that philosophy is concerned with statements or, more specifically, with statements about statements. It is with this presupposition that I shall begin.

I

PROPOSITION 1: *Philosophy issues in statements about statements*. It is, in other words, "discourse about discourse" or, simply, analysis of sign-contexts in their syntactical, semantical or pragmatical dimensions. Three decisions, far-reaching yet not explicitly argued for, are entailed by this declaration: 1) philosophy is not only essentially but also exhaustively a cognitive discipline; 2) as a cognitive discipline it is discursive; 3) as a discursive type of knowledge it cannot be about object-events (in which case it would become science or common-sense) but it must be about the discourse of the formal and empirical sciences, *i.e.*, discourse about their discourse.

A case can be made for alternatives to these three decisions. A possibly exhaustive list of such alternatives could be set up by taking account of the various combinations that result from the distinction of philosophical objectives (discursive knowledge, non-discursive knowledge, "ways of life") and the various means for achieving these objectives (discursive knowledge about either linguistic or non-linguistic subject-matter, non-discursive knowledge, by itself or in conjunction with discursive knowledge, about linguistic or non-linguistic subject-matter). Thus, against 1) the conception of philosophy as a purely cognitive enterprise, thinkers, both Western and Eastern, have held with varying emphasis on the instrumental importance of knowledge, to the philosophical objective as a way of life, the cultivation of attitudes leading to acceptance at least, to bliss at best, of and within a world which, in important respects, is locked to human understanding.

As against 2), the essentially discursive nature of philosophical knowledge, some Occidental and many more Oriental philosophers have been skeptical about the effective range of verbalization concerning a type of knowledge deemed most essential to man. Thus, when Sekito, a master of Zen, was asked by a monk: "What is that which makes up your self?" Sekito replies: "What do you want from me?" When the monk insists: "If I do not ask you, where can I get the solution?" the reply is: "Did you ever loose it?" [2]. What is illustrated here could be generalized in this manner: a) there is some knowledge which requires silence rather than discourse to come into being; b) such silence is itself only one condition for an active mode of non-discursive knowing directed not towards the readily named sense-data of the external world but to data open only to concentrated self-reflection; c) the evidential nature of this self-reflexive concentration involves confirmation and testing through living in time which, in some of its phases, lends itself neither to verbalization as a means nor to verbalization of its outcome.

An Oriental counter-positivist could conceivably argue against the exclusively discursive approach of much Western philosophizing and insist that the "life-testing" of a philosophy is as severe as, if not more difficult than, the "fact-testing" of scientific theorizing. Such "life-testing" is altogether neglected by those philosophers whose activities are exhausted in "discourse about discourse". Supposing, however, that, suspending argument on this point, we reassert the essentially cognitive and discursive function of *Western* Philosophy, are we thereby also committed to hold 3), that its concern must be restricted to the discourse of formal and scientific languages? Occidental philosophy surely has rarely lived up to this requirement, even though some of its representatives engaged in linguistically illuminating analyses long before this occupation was singled out as the sole defining trait of all philosophical work.

The declaration that philosophy "should" be discourse about discourse has been recommended as a rule for two reasons: 1) it is said to lead to a clarification of different areas of cognitive responsibility by precluding philosophers from competing with scientists who alone may pronounce about the properties of the natural and social order; 2) as initiating analysis of linguistic meaning, philosophy can render a service not performed by other disciplines, namely the explication of logical and semantical assumptions and the attendant resolution of ambiguities to which those who use, but do not analyze, language are forever prone.

These are important tasks for the philosopher; but are they exhaustive of his concern? I think not, if only for the reason that some of the most pregnant cognitive objectives can be reduced neither to the level of linguistic analysis nor to that of the special sciences. Both practical and theoretical considerations suggest the need for a discipline which can bring the selective evidence of both discursive and non-discursive knowledge to bear on the elucidation of problems and concepts which are at once the most perennial and timely, the most personal and universal to confront man. Far from competing with the scientist, the philosopher's cultural function is that of the generalizer of and mediator between competing knowledge-claims. He must move therefore on a level of generality for which the various scientific and non-scientific reality-accountings at best can only furnish the data for more inclusive concerns. He will accordingly have to formulate hypothess which cut across both discursive and non-discursive sign-contexts. These integrative hypotheses, finally, must be as compatible with the findings of the special disciplines as these findings themselves must be compatible with the various kinds of evidence appropriate to and available within these speciaal (scientific or non-scientific) sign-contexts themselves. We conclude that a conception of philosophy as "issuing in statements about statements" is either not entailed by the semiotic scheme under discussion or that it must be interpreted more generously to allow for a much richer view of philosophical work than is envisaged by its positivist proponents.

With these critical comments upon what I take to be the implicit premise of Reichenbach's restriction of the semiotic range of philosophy, I turn now to a discussion of the first "conclusion" which is said to "follow immediately from an analysis of modern science". (See above, page 146).

II

PROPOSITION 2: *Knowledge divides into synthetic and analytic statements.* Statements, to be meaningful, must be certifiable as either valid by syntactical rules or as (probably) true by rules of empirical designation. Knowledge, in other words, occurs only within the formal and semantical sign-contexts specified by the semiotic scheme. The methodological value of this declaration is perhaps incontestable. Its recognition entails the elaboration of rules and of procedures appropriate for the testing of characteristically distinct knowledge-claims. But exactly what knowledge-claim is made by a declaration which not only distinguishes syntactical from semantical meaning but which also prescribes that no other type of meaning can lay claim to being cognitive? The declaration that all knowledge is either analytic or synthetic would itself have to be certified as either one or the other. If synthetic, *i. e.* factually meaningful, it would also be false in the face of the great multitude of pronouncements, believed to be cognitive and yet not susceptible to testing by the positivist model of scientific designation. If analytic, the declaration that all knowledge, unless formal, *must* be testable according to rules of designation is analytic clearly of only one particular type of knowledge, namely the scientific type. It is legislative for any knowledge only with the additional value-assumption that scientifically warranted knowledge alone is worth having or worthy of the title "knowledge". (see p. 140)

Such preference for the value of scientific knowledge, however, must remain groundless for philosophers who also hold that a "cognitive ethics is impossible". It could neither be derived analytically within a value-scheme nor factually from an examination of the beliefs held to be cognitive by men, whether positivists or not. To be sure, the thesis that knowledge is either formal or verifiable by statements of fact and, if verifiable, then also more reliable (with respect to facts) than knowledge not reducible to such verification, can be raised to the status of being analytically true of empirical science. But then there are the knowledge-claims of the arts, ethics, religions and metaphysics. The criteria of factually-designative meaning, germane to the sciences, obviously cannot accommodate these candidates for cognitive meaning. On the other hand, nothing is gained by calling them unscientific and thus depriving them of a title to which, as a rule, they never aspired. The philosophical task still remains so to modify or interpret formal and designative criteria of meaning that other than scientific versions of synthetic knowledge can be accounted for in the formal and factual sign-contexts of the semiotic scheme.

III

What then about Reichenbach's next conclusions, drawn for the semiotic range of philosophy from his understanding of modern science? I shall formulate them as Propositions 3–5 and deal with them separately.

PROPOSITION 3: *Synthetic statements inform us about matters of fact.* In other words, factually meaningful statements either refer directly or are reducible to statements referring directly to events occurring in space and time. Stated in terms of the semiotic scheme, events, functioning as tokens of symbols in language, are true or false with respect to object-events if the assertion of the former corresponds to the occurrence of the latter according to rules laid down for natural languages by syntactical and semantical rules of grammar and vocabulary or, for scientific languages, by procedures (formal or operational), specified by methodology. "Truth", in other words, is defined here as a property of some statements; of those, that is, which conform to rules, either given in the semantics of an object-language or as given by scientific decisions for the testing of precise reference of symbol-events to object-events.

On this account, signs as symbols function as successors to the "universals", "ideas" or "concepts" of traditional philosophy. They are artifact-events, endowed by conventional decisions, to name properties, things or relations. The particular event-occurrence, "dated" with respect to both place and time, happens only once; it becomes "known" as an instance of a property, or as a member of a class or series determined by the property, which is named by the symbol. To say therefore that "synthetic statements inform us about matters of fact" is to say that statements,

as sets of symbols, are evaluated as "true" or "false" with respect
to the (physical and technical) possibility of perceptually en-
countering particular events recognized as instances of the properties named. The "problem of knowledge" now turns out to be
a pseudo-problem; concepts or universals are words; and words,
as symbols, are moored to events via coordination rules of language or methodology.

On second thought, however, at least two problems are sup-
pressed in this seemingly lucid version of relating symbols to
events. For one thing, is a relation of sign-events (symbols) to
object-events (particulars) even conceivable? Of the two relata,
one, by definition, must endure in time and for some time; the
other cannot. Events, like their historical predecessors, the
"particulars", can have only one, vaguely delimited, space-time
occurrence. This means that signs cannot be coordinated as
names of properties or relations to events unless events can be
recognized as instances of such properties or relations. The possibility of this recognition, however, requires that the fleeting
stream of events can hold still, as it were, long enough to permit
perception of relatively stable event-sets. This requirement, it
turns out, is met by the recognition of a perceptual sign-context
in which, according to Berkeley, sensations "mutually signify
each other" [3], and where, according to William James, some sens-
ed events are "selected by experience" to become the "bearers of
reality" while others function as "mere signs and suggestions
of these" [4]. (see p. 105)

The specification of the mechanisms involved in this mode of
perceptual sign-functioning has been under investigation for
some time now by experimental, comparative and Gestalt psychologists. The philosophical relevance of their findings has, as a
rule, not been appreciated by philosophical sign-analysers before
Cassirer. These findings are relevant because they do help to
make intelligible the otherwise puzzling notion of a "reference"
or "application" of signs as rules, concepts or theories, frankly recognized as "symbolic", to an allegedly non-symbolic, brute, in-
stantaneous reality of events, particulars or sense-data. The
psychological immediacy of perceptual apprehension is one thing,
the sign-mediated character of the perceptually encountered
event-classes is another. Our semiotic scheme should therefore

be amended to read that syntactical, semantical or pragmatical rules always refer to "classes of events", interpreted
symbolically as qualities, thing-properties or relations, and not
to events as fleeting and singular bits of a non-signifying realm
of being.

Secondly, even as amended above, *Proposition 3* still raises
problems. To define events or event-classes by the property of
"occurring in space and time" is to name a context distinct both
from the perceptual sign-context of the event-classes of which
this property holds and also from either conventionally formal or
factually designative sign-contexts. The property of "occurring
in space and time" defines by itself a class, namely the class of all
event-classes of which factual properties can be predicated. The
categorial space-time context is thus presupposed in any definition of an event-class. It signifies a symbolic context neither
itself perceived nor identifiable as a conventionally syntactical
or factually descriptive context.

Philosophical analysis thus must distinguish between classe-
of events, perceived as "particulars" and the "class of particsu
lars" which is exhaustively defined by the property of space-time
occurrence. We have, in other words, a "particularity" (flux,
becoming, matter, etc.) as the class of all event-classes which
satisfy the condition of occurring in space-time and also the
"particular event" as an instance of being thus determinable.
What is the point of this distinction? If it holds, then quite different relations are involved in the reference of signs to particular
event-classes on one hand and to the class of all such event-classes, the realm of the particulars, on the other.

Consider once more the definition of a particular (event-class
as perceived) as "what must occur in space and time". Both
"space" and "time", in the language of semiotics, are "general
words", signs which name the property that categorially determines an event-context presupposed by all contexts of semantic
designation. If this is so, then there arises, besides the linguistic
analysis of the way in which signs can refer to events, the more
controversial analysis of the manner in which this semantical
coordination can be justified. Clearly, such justification cannot
be given in terms of rules whereby this or that particular sign is
to be related to this or that event-class according to semantic

conventions. Instead, we here face the not so recent epistemological problem of accounting for this possibility.

The philosophical tradition, to the extent that it has been sensitive to this issue, has attempted to make intelligible the reference of signs (general words, ideas, forms, universals, concepts etc.) to event-classes (particulars, sense-data, perceptions, objects, etc.) by either making the necessary assumptions about the constitution (order, dimension, structure, patterns, etc.) of reality (being, cosmos, world, nature, etc.) or about the constitution and function of the sign-interpretant (soul, mind, reason, understanding, etc.) or both. I take it that some contemporary philosophers and most semioticians read the lessons of this tradition as rather discouraging with respect to an adequate solution for this problem. In this case, it seems, one would either have to deliver a more adequate account of one's own or to confess frankly one's commitment to the ontological assumption of "order", "regularity" or "limited variability" in the form of a postulate which is presupposed by, but not itself part of, any conventional system of syntax or semantics. At any rate, to deny the adequacy of traditional ontologies is one thing, to deny the challenge of a problem which stands in need of some accounting is quite another thing.

IV

PROPOSITION 4: *Analytic statements are empty.* If by an analytic statement be understood a formula the validity of which is independent of the truth-values of its components or, in Carnap's version, as not designative of things but significant only with respect to (the syntax of) language, it must indeed be empty in the sense of not naming events. For the same reason, however, analytic statements alone can lay claim to hold with necessity, and, vice versa, all necessary propositions are analytic proposition conditional only upon the endorsement of rules. Thus, all necessary propositions are conventional within the sign-context of rules within which they are assertible.

Since the property of necessity attaches to propositions not in isolation nor in their coordination to events but only to their relatability with other propositions, it is a function of rules adopted within a system of rules. Recognizing this conventional character of "necessary truths", semioticians have not only succeeded in interpreting mathematical systems as syntactical ones; they have also drawn the conclusion that logic, like mathematics, encompasses several equally necessary alternative systems. Aristotelian logic, like Euclidean geometry, now appears as a special case, privileged only in the sense that it lends itself better than alternative formal systems to such interpretations as appear fruitful for certain cognitive purposes. This conventional conception of logic raises difficulties at least as regards the status of such principles as those of identity, non-contradiction and excluded middle.

It can be shown that the principles of logic, referred to as the "three laws of thought", enjoy a necessity which is not conventional in the same sense which qualifies other syntactically necessary propositions. It has been suggested that this is so because these three principles define any and all formal systems as "systems" since they explicate the meaning of consistency which itself is a logical condition for any set of rules to become a system of rules. Accordingly, it can be said that any logical system which aims to undertake a derivation of these principles in terms of other primitive assumptions must presuppose their employment if the attempted derivation is to be a logically consistent, i.e. true derivation.

It would seem to follow that at least some formal laws must be accredited with being necessarily true in the sense of being presupposed by, rather than conventionally determined within, any given formal system. Now, since all formally possible systems must conform to some logically necessary laws, and since some formal systems can be interpreted as descriptively applicable to events, it follows that at least some logically necessary laws apply to any descriptively meaningful discourse about events. One consequence of this conclusion would be another proposition to the effect that these logical principles, not provable within logic but presupposed by all logically consistent discourse about events, cannot be out of conformity to some basic order-characteristics of that realm of events referred to as "reality".

In order to escape this terrifying conclusion, proponents of a "logic without ontology" (e.g. Ernest Nagel) have suggested that the peculiar character of the laws of thought could be illuminated by regarding them merely as pragmatic requirements for effective inquiry. Various proposals to this effect can perhaps be summarized in this manner: inquiries into the behavior of men engaged in inquiry and in the communication of the results of these inquiries, disclose that such behavior is effective only if it respects the prescriptions formalized in the principles of identity, non-contradiction and excluded middle. These principles are therefore "analytic" of effective inquiry and communication and, instead of reflecting features of reality, they merely reflect conditions for communication without confusion. Since the final resolution of the epistemological and ontological problems involved in the determination of the status of logical laws transcends the ambitions of this chapter, it may be sufficient to point to a number of considerations which render questionable the thesis that the necessity attaching to the laws of thought is fully intelligible when interpreted merely as a regulative requirement for meaningful discourse.

To ground the conventionality of logical principles upon their pragmatic usefulness for the behavior of men engaged in inquiry is to assert the non sequitur that what is regulative for inquiry cannot, for that reason, also be a cue to some of the structural properties of the non-linguistic referent of all inquiries.

To ground the conventionality of logical principles upon their bearing for language rather than upon the "structure of reality" is to leave unaccounted the circumstance that only some languages are fit for cognitive discourse about events and that no language is fit for it unless it conforms to logical principles. It is true, of course, that these principles function only as necessary and not also as sufficient conditions for any language to be descriptively meaningful of non-linguistic events. To exhibit even this type of conditionality, however, requires the further assumption that what is invariably appropriate for descriptive language cannot be entirely unconnected with what a language is about when it yields description rather than mere expression.

To ground the conventionality of the laws of thought upon the consideration that they are required only by such languages as can lay claim to be "adequate" for cognitive purposes is to certify their necessity with reference to human concerns rather than to any "order of events". But what does "adequacy" mean here? If the logical principles in question are formally adequate as invariable conditions for any language that can claim to be empirically descriptive and if, furthermore, any language, to be adequate to the cognitive purposes of men, must conform to these principles, then it would seem that these purposes, to be satisfied rather than frustrated, could hardly be served by principles which are in no wise reflective of the order of what is the common referent of all cognitively meaningful discourse [5].

If it were thinkable to make the assumption that reality is a chaos rather than an order of events which exhibits distinguishable invariances, then the necessity of assuming principles of identity and non-contradiction for the purpose of inquiring into its features would be unwarranted. On the other hand, to require these principles not for specific inquiries but for any inquiry is tantamount to admitting that they cannot be conventional in the sense in which less universal laws or generalizations can be said to be moored to pragmatical, semantical or syntactical conventions. At least one of the criteria of an empirically "adequate" language concerns its capacity to be descriptive of extra-linguistic events. To the extent that all descriptions are selective and, at best, probable accounts rather than complete and certain ones, no correspondence between language and events and no reflection of the "order of events" in the order discernible in discourse can be taken for granted. To the extent, however, that some languages are communicative of extra-linguistic events with some degree of certainty, and could not even be partially successful for cognitive purposes unless in conformity to the laws of logic, these laws themselves cannot be conventional in any of the senses recognized by the positivist semiotician. We conclude that, in terms of our semiotic scheme, there are at least some and possibly more analytic statements belonging to the dimension of formal sign-contexts which, while "empty" of empirical determination, are not any more or less "related to reality" than is any pervasive symbol-perspective which man can take of it.

V

PROPOSITION 5: *The modern analysis of knowledge makes a cognitive ethics impossible.* This, in Reichenbach's argumnet, follows from propositions 2 to 4. To be sure, if all knowledge is either synthetic or analytic and, if analytic then also empty, then, if it is empty of empirical relevance, it is also incapable of grounding universally binding moral laws. In so far as knowledge is synthetic, however, it can at best yield statements descriptive of the actual behavior of men and not be prescriptive or directive of the way men ought to behave. It follows that statements, proposed as both universally binding and yet directive, cannot be propositions at all since their joint possession of both characteristics would preclude their classification as either syntactically or semantically meaningful propositions. In other words: statements containing value-predicates can become propositions only if they are interpreted as state-descriptions of the valuing individuals. In this case they are, like other descriptive statements, nondirective for other individuals. Or they are offered as proposals, directive for some (or all) individuals. Then they are, or are derived from, expressions of preferences, commitments, decisions and thus "irrational" in the sense that a language, containing such expressions, can be neither true nor false with respect to them, and in the further sense that they cannot be analytically grounded in laws governing the nature of reality, man or society.

Since the property of "irrationality" is always relative to an implicit scheme of rationality, our attempt to make a case for the relevance of knowledge in connection with the expression and direction of value-realizations can in principle take the form either of challenging a scheme that cannot account for this connection or of challenging the denial that value-expressions can be accommodated in a semiotic scheme. I shall argue on the second alternative.

I submit that whether one entertains a proposition A ("I either marry her or not") or a proposition B ("I marry her") or a proposition C ("I had better marry her"), all three expressions are equally "irrational", *i. e.*, meaningless in independence from a set of rules, be they syntactical, semantical or moral.

In the case of proposition B, it is true that, depending upon which rule-context I choose, I can either derive it as a conclusion or make it serve as a premise. The same holds true, however, for proposition C.

The difference between the relations of implication as they

hold respectively for either empirical generalizations or ethical premises and moral rules does not concern the character of necessity involved in both, but rather the terminal points or ultimate premises to which they can be attached. It would seem, therefore, that the "irrationality" of value-premises cannot be squared with the rationally necessary relations into which they can enter. Some philosophers have held, accordingly, that only those value-statements are "irrational" which serve as *axioms* of implicative relations, *i.e.* as statements of final ends or ultimate commitments. But so, one should think, do all ultimate assumptions.

If there is a difference between the basic assumptions of the sciences on one hand and of moral systems on the other, it would seem to concern our disposition to envisage less readily alternative systems of physics than of ethics. The considerations, however, upon which such different envisagement would be grounded are at best historical ones and neither logical nor scientific. Scientific principles, to be sure, have been and may again be replaced by alternate ones. Some ethical principles, however, have proven remarkably pervasive and, where subject to change, they have been sensitive to the changing conceptions which the physical, biological, psychological and social sciences have offered for the interpretation of human nature and the conditions under which it can be realized. At this point, one must note that just as any assertion can become a scientific proposition only if it can become part of a system of already established descriptive laws, so any preference-statement can become a morally significant proposition only if it can become part of an already established or endorsed system of ends.

Systems of descriptive laws and systems of prescriptive laws can be shown to be connected along both descriptive and prescriptive lines. Just as moral ends are related to conceptions of human nature based on descriptive knowledge about man and his world, so man's knowledge about anything whatever is related to such prescriptions as consistency and reliability of discourse.

The belief, as seemingly obvious as false, that the same data allow of only one set of descriptively correct interpretations but of various non-compatible prescriptive evaluations will have to be abandoned in the light of a more rigorous examination of

the different meanings of "sameness" involved in the characterization of the data as the referents of description and prescription
respectively. The apparent gap, stressed by ethical relativists,
between the "same" situations or actions on one hand and the
great cultural variety of their moral evaluations on the other will
be bridged as soon as some of their connecting links can be specified. Investigations by anthropologists and social psychologists
may prove illuminating on this point. Once attention is directed
to the circumstance that the apparently arbitrary relation between
the seeming identity of situations and the variety of culturally
possible interpretations of them is mediated by the perception
of different aspects and within different frames of cognitive orientation, a more rational comprehension of value-schemes should
become possible. As we shall be able to account for the perceptual
and cognitive factors which operate between physical situations
as encountered and human situations as perceived, valued and
evaluated, the positivist thesis of an independent variability
between "facts" and "values" islikely to give way to a more
adequate recognition of the co-variability not only between the
facts as situationally perceived and culturally evaluated, but also
between the available objective knowlededge about nature and
society on one hand and the formulation of moral objectives on
the other. Aristotle knew a long time ago that "fire burns both
in Hellas and in Persia, but men's ideas of right and wrong vary
from place to place". Yet this historical generalization neither
encouraged him to consider all ideas about what is right as equally
"right", nor did it discourage him from writing the *Nicomachean
Ethics*.

We conclude therefore that, in terms of our semiotic scheme,
human concerns about human ends are, in principle, as amenable
to rule-directed rationality as are human concerns about the
events of human and non-human environment. Note that on
both the formal validity and the factual truth levels, we refer to
event-classes (tokens, objects, persons, etc.) as well as to rules,
syntactical or semantical, with respect to which assertions are
evaluated as being in conformity or not. If conformity is maintained, we speak validly or truly. Analogous conformity demands
also hold for discourse about human concerns and purposes. An
experience of pleasure, reverence or positive affectivity can

be asserted as valuable only under the acknowledged or tacit assumption of a symbolic context of rules. Value-ascriptions to such event-classes can neither be made (morally) nor themselves evaluated (ethically) except as conformity to rules, functioning as criteria of evaluation, is specified.

As regards this specification, philosophers have taken essentially three approaches: they have either endorsed moral rules as made available by the secular or religious tradition of their own or an earlier time; or they have selected from those rules only such as they could also derive (justify) from such concepts of man or the state as were consonant with their theories of nature, God or knowledge; or, finally, as moral transvaluators, they have expounded new rules in conformity with objectives more germane to their respective conceptions of man and the good life.

Formalization of this field has not gone far as yet. Kant, whose work is a pioneer attempt to provide formal criteria to be satisfied by any rule if it is to be a moral one, has often been misunderstood, and occasionally misunderstood himself, to have offered an alternative to concrete moral rules. The Hedonists, on the other side, to whose orientation contemporary semioticians gravitate most noticeably, have suggested that the touchstone of moral rules is to be sought in experiences of pleasure or affectivity. The history of Western philosophy, from Plato to Whitehead, supplies an almost uninterrupted and negative comment upon all attempts to ground decisions between pleasures and pains or between pleasures and pleasures upon "finer", "greater" or "better" pleasures without the adoption of additional criteria for so distinguishing them. From the perspective of our semiotic scheme, pleasure-events, like object-events, are interpreted in terms of rules which are recommended as rational on the basis of their derivability from, or compatibility with, such concepts of natural or social order as are cognitively persuasive to the ethical thinker. To be sure, testing for the cash-value of pleasure, in some form and at some time, must be recognized as just as necessary a condition for any evaluation as testing for perceptual data is required for any empirically significant assertion. But what is being tested in both cases are not the event-classes of perception or pleasure but theories about either nature or the good life.

VI

Validity, Truth, Value: Their Interrelation. The preceding comments are intended to limit the claims of a currently influential interpretation of a semiotic scheme which I hold to be philosophically more valuable than the orientation of thought which brought it forth. With the provisions suggested in my critical comments upon Reichenbach's formulation of that orientation, I conclude that the contexts of syntactical, semantical and axiological meaning circumscribe the area of philosophical work with respect to discourse. The remaining comments will be directed towards exhibiting the interrelation of these three contexts of signification.

Value-statements, to be statements, must conform to syntactical rules of discourse. They will imply, exclude or be compatible with each other. Transformation-rules, if desired, could be formalized. Thus, for a given axiological scheme, to attribute value to an event-class A (say "material goods") implies attributing value to sub-sets or other event-classes B (say "money") but not to C (say "scarcity").

To be statements, valuations must also conform to semantical rules. They will name classes of events as referents of value-terms. Designation-rules, if desired, could also be formalized. To attribute moral value to an event-class M is to assert that its presence or activation directly or indirectly, potentially or actually, positively or negatively is related to other event-classes (pleasure, reverence, positive affectivity, etc.) in a manner which is in conformity with the ends and in accordance with the rules specified within a moral system. In science, the assertion of descriptive statements is controlled by both conventional(deductive) and non-conventional (perceptual) testing factors. In the field of evaluation also, statements must conform to both conventional (axiological) and non-conventional (affectivity) testing factors. To discover, understand and test a scientific assertion involves accordingly both a comprehension of the comparatively complex inferential procedures and the employment of normally functioning sense-organs. The first condition is satisfied only by the expert; almost anybody can satisfy the sceond one. Analogously: to discover, understand and test an evaluation requires comprehension of the (less complex) inferential procedures involved in determining the standard-compatibility of the consequences of actions and, beyond the mere employment of normally functioning sense-organs, also the whole range of sensitive and imaginative response to all the shadings of humanly significant events. By confining their testing procedures to publicly accessible perceptual reports, scientific assertions can attain to greater interpersonal reliability. Value-assertions, however, while less reliable in that sense, make up for the shortcoming by greater scope, and comprise truth-correctness as only one among other human concerns.

The difficulty in the path of scientifically reliable reference to events is the inferential factor. Educational emphasis must accordingly be on the instruction in methods and procedures. The difficulty in the path of sound evaluations is the testing factor. Educational emphasis must accordingly be on the gradual maturing of discriminating sensitivity.

Just as evaluations involve syntactical consistency- and semantical reference-rules, so do rules of discourse involve decision-problems. There is no resolution to a decision-problem, however, except with reference to such purposes as consistency, comprehensiveness and testability in general, and to such more specific purposes as may best be realized by deciding for one set of semiotic conventions rather than for another. Purposes, it has been said, are in the end "behind" all rules of language. Some naturalists have suggested that if purposes are indeed back of all discourse, rational or otherwise, they are themselves backed by the "exigencies of life". To speak of the control of purposes by life, or perhaps better, by the life-requirements of humans in a human or a non-human world, has meant, as a rule, that this control is either irrational in the sense of involving causes rather than reasons, or metaphysical in the sense of involving the ultimate structure of reality.

Since to talk about causes in independence of reasons for establishing causal connections is cognitively as frustrating as to assume an unknowable structure of reality, a somewhat more sophisticated version of the thesis that all purposes, values and truths are controlled by the life-requirements of human beings has proposed "survival" as the final criterion for judging the adequacy or success of all cognitive and valuational schemes of orientation. Unfortunately, the concept of survival is never applicable to schemes that exist in the present and, by their sheer existence, disclose their survival. As a criterion for determining successful schemes of the past, the survival-concept is notoriously vague and misleading. The past, after all, never does exhibit surviving systems of belief in independence from contexts of impinging forces, some favorable to their survival, others not. We are left, therefore, with the realization that some belief-systems, under "favorable" conditions, survived and, since "favorable" refers to all conditions whatever which go with "surviving" systems, history would indeed seem to teach us the inescapable lesson that belief-systems which could survive, survived. The explanatory value of the survival concept, therefore, is at best minimal since it in no wise directs the search for such factors as may be found to have bearing upon the continued existence of human schemes of orientation. It is perhaps not a matter for argument that there are non-discursive factors which exercise a rather effective, though flexible, control in supporting some but not all of the discursive schemes which have been developed for the realization of human purposes. [6]

It is exactly one of the defining tasks of the cognitive branches of such schemes of orientation to recognize those factors that may be crucial for the survival of those who entertain them. Yet, the discernment of these factors, however tentative, presupposes the realization of those values which control all cognitively effective behavior of man. Thus, consistency and reliability of discourse are values precisely because conformity to their prescriptions is a necessary, though not sufficient, condition for the realization of other values. It is for this reason that schemes of orientation which do include these theoretic values have proven more likely to meet the life-requirements and purposes (however differently conceived) of men than schemes which do not.

Whatever knowledge is acquired, whatever perspectives are taken, in whatever language, they surely must be such as to render feasible the realization of at least some human purposes. To admit this, however, is not to leave the specification of what purposes are worth realizing to an indefinite dynamics of life. To hold that rules of formal or factual discourse are controlled by purposes does not necessitate the conclusion that, upon reaching the stratum of purposes, we encounter a realm more basic than tentative human discourse, value and belief and at the same time independent of these. As in the case of any good postulate, the postulation of "basic human purposes" or "life-requirements" must warrant its status in terms of internally consistent, empirically possible and value-enhancing schemes which are derivable at best, compatible at least, with its assumption. The selection of some purposes as basic or ultimate is itself dependently variable with the concepts of nature and human nature that are formulated within different symbolic schemes at various stages of cognitive and valuational orientation.

The argument can now be summarized. I have started with the suggestion of a semiotic framework whose formal, factual and valuational sign-contexts I take to be exhaustive of philosophy as discourse. I have tried to stress the potential scope of this framework by questioning what seem to me unwarranted strictures proposed by most contemporary semioticians. The interrelation of the three dimensions of discourse was emphasized to indicate their joint sufficiency and irreducibility either to any indefinite concepts of "life" and "survival" or to any dogmatically definite concepts of "Nature" or "Being".

I conclude: (1) We can construct a syntax of value-schemes as readily (in principle) as a syntax of formal discourse or a syntax of the deductive portions of empirical knowledge. (2) We are dealing with event-classes in all three contexts, be they the tokens of symbols in discourse, be they the referents of factual discourse, or be they the referents of human concerns. (3) We are dealing with values in all three contexts, be it the value of consistency, be it the value of reliability, or be it the context in which all values, besides these, become the object of rational concern.

BIBLIOGRAPHICAL NOTES

INTRODUCTION

[1] So far translated: Vol I. *Language*, Yale University Press, New Haven, 1953; Vol II. *Myth, ibid.*, 1954. Untranslated: Vol III, German title *Phaenomenology der Erkenntnis*, Verlag Bruno Cassirer, Berlin, 1929

[2] Translated by W. C. Swabey, Chicago, Open Court Publishing Co, 1923; re-published by Dover Press, 1954

[3] Yale University Press, New Haven, 1944

[4] Yale University Press, New Haven, 1946

[5] Translated by S. Langer, New York, Harper & Brothers, 1946

[6] Translated by Gutman, Kristeller and Randall, Princeton University Press, 1945

[7] Yale University, New Haven, 1950

[8]) A comprehensive bibliography (up to 1949) was prepared by the author (and W Solmitz) in: The Library of Living Philosophers; Vol. VI (Cassirer); pp 881–910.

CHAPTER I

[1] in the preface to Vol III of *Philosophie der Symbolischen Formen*; see fragment "'Spirit' and 'Life' in Contemporary Philosophy", in *Library of Living Philosophy*, Vol VI, p. 857–880

[2] *The Sophist*: 242

[3] *Metaphysics*, Book A, vii; Ross translation

[4] John Dewey, *Reconstruction in Philosophy*, chapters 1 and 5

[5] *PhdSF*, III, p 6

[6] *Language and Myth*, pp 44, 45

[7] *Substance and Function*, ch. I

[8] *Journal of Philosophy*, XXXIX, No 12, p 311

[9] *ibid.*, p 312

[10] *Metaphysics and the New Logic*, Univ. of Chicago Press, 1946, p 77

[11] *Opuscules et fragments inédits*; ed. Couturat, p 27

[12] Gerhardt: *Hauptschriften*, Vol IV, p 18

[13] *Opuscules*, p 18

[14] *ibid.*, p 374

[15] "Quod sit idea", in *Hauptschriften*, Vol VII, p 263

[16] *Mathematische Schriften*, Vol. V, p 141

[17] *Hauptschriften*, Vol. VI, p 568

[18] Book IV, chapter iv, par. 14

[19] Chapter 9, par. 21

[20] Chapter I, par. 5

[21] Descartes, *Meditationes*, Book V

[22] *Essay*, Book III, chapter 2, par. 5

[23] *Das Erkenntnisproblem*, Vol. II, pp 227–390

[24] *Essay*, Book III, chapter 1, par. 3

[25] *A Treatise Concerning the Principles of Human Understanding*, Introduction, par. 21

[26] *Dialogues between Hylas and Philonous*, I

[27] *Siris*, pp 338, 345, etc.

[28] *PhdSF*, Vol. II, p 5

[29] *Principles etc.* par. 89

[30] *ibid.*, par 110
[31] *PhdSF*, Vol III, p 4
[32] T. D. Weldon, *Introduction to Kant's Critique of Pure Reason*, p 77
[33] *ibid.*
[34] *Das Erkenntnisproblem*, Vol. III, pp 3/4
[35] *Prolegomena*, par. 4
[36] *Das Erkenntnisproblem*, Vol II, p 665
[37] *Kritik der reinen Vernunft*, Einleitung, par. vii
[38] *Prolegomena*, par. 38
[39] *Kritik d.r.V.*; Transc. Elementarlehre, par 1
[40] Vol III, p 314
[41] *Kant's Theorie der Erfahrung*, 3rd ed., p 242
[42] *PhdSF*, Vol III, p 13
[43] *Language and Myth*, p 8
[44] *ibid.*
[45] *History of Western Philosophy*, p 701
[46] in *Idee und Gestalt*, pp 35–65
[47] *Kritik d.r.V.*; Transc. Deduktion, par. 26
[48] *PhdSF*, Vol. I, p 10

CHAPTER II

[1] *Power and Events*, p xv
[2] p 16
[3] pp 16/17
[4] *Theoria: Tidskrift for Filosofi och Psykologi*, Vol 11, p 158
[5] *PhdSF*, Vol. I, p 13
[6] p 237
[7] Axel Hagerstroem, *Eine Studie zur Schwedischen Philosophie der Gegenwart*, Ch. I.
[8] *ibid.*
[9] *ibid.*
[10] *PhdSF*, Vol I, p 11
[11] *An Essay on Man*, p 70
[12] *Zur Logik der Kulturwissenschaften Fuenf Studien*, Göteborg, 1942, p 94
[31] *Theoria*, 1938, p 173
[14] Against a narrowly behavioristic interpretation, see the author's "Theory of Learning and Culture-Concept" in: Philosophy of Science; Vol 21, No 4, pp 344-347. (Oct. 1954)

CHAPTER III

[1] *PhdSF*, Vol III, p 109
[2] *PhdSF*, Vol III, p 475; also *Substance & Function*, p 143
[3] *Foundations of Logic and Mathematics*, p 4
[4] *Procedures of Empirical Science*, Univ. of Chicago Press, 1938, p 4
[5] *ibid.*, p 5
[6] *PhdSF*, Vol III, p 109
[7] *PhdSF*, Vol III, p 380
[8] *PhdSF*, Vol III, p 85
[9] *PhdSF*, Vol II, p 52
[10] *PhdSF*, Vol III, p 85
[11] *Experience and Nature*, p 96
[12] *PhdSF*, Vol III, p 85
[13] *PhdSF*, Vol III, p 165
[14] *PhdSF*, Vol III, p 160
[15] *An Analysis of Knowledge and Valuation*, p 14

[16] *PhdSF*, Vol III, p 148
[17] *PhdSF*, Vol III, p 330
[18] *ibid.*, p 214
[19] *PhdSF*, Vol III, p 346
[20] *Substance and Function*, p 223
[21] *PhdSF*, Vol III, p 350
[22] "A class is an incomplete symbol- all its members must be thought of as variables of a propositional function". Whitehead and Russell, *Principia Mathematica* Vol II, p 75
[23] *Substance and Function*, p 25
[24] *PhdSF*, Vol III, p 351
[25] *ibid.*
[26] *Principles of Mathematics*, VII, p 85

CHAPTER IV

[1] *Theoria*, 1936, pp 279–332
[2] *ibid.*, p 291
[3] *ibid.*, p 292
[4] e.g. in *PhdSF*, Vol. III, p 447
[5] *Theoria*, 1936, p 331
[6] *ibid.*, 1938, pp 145–175
[7] Cohen and Nagel, *Introduction to Logic and Scientific Method*, p 135
[8] *Theoria*, 1938, p 169
[9] *Substance and Function*, p 101
[10] *Theoria*, 1938, p 169
[11] p 93
[12] *Theoria*, 1938, p 151
[13] *Die Krise der Psychologie*, Jena, 1928, p 97
[14] par. 4
[15] *Grundzüge einer Lehre vom Lichtsinn*, par. 4
[16] *Handbuch der Physiologischen Optik*, 1896, p 607
[17] *PhdSF*, Vol I, p 32
[18] *PhdSF*, Vol III, p 157
[19] *Theoria*, 1939, p 153
[20] *Zeitschrift für Aesthetik*, XXI, p 195; *PhdSF*, Vol III, p 231; *Theoria*, 1938, p 154
[21] *Theoria*, 1938, p 155–156
[22] *PhdSF*, Vol I, p 31

CHAPTER V

[1] *Notae in programma quoddam*; ed. Adam-Tannery, Vol. VII, p 360
[2] *Principles etc.*, par. 53
[3] *PhdSF*, Vol III, p 172
[4] e.g. E. R. Hilgard, *Theories of Learning*, NY, 1948
[5] "Topology and Hodological Space", in M. Marx, *Psychological Theories*, NY, 1951, p 233
[6] O. Kleinberg, *Social Psychology*, NY, 1940, chapter viii
[7] M. Sherif, "An Experimental Approach to the Study of Attitudes", in *Sociometry*, 1937, Vol I, p 90–98
[8] O. Spengler, *Decline of the West*, NY, 1943, p 179
[9] *PhdSF*, Vol III, p vi–vii
[10] *Handbook of the American Indian Languages*, p 43
[11] C. and W. Stern, *Die Kindersprache*, Leipzig, 1920, p 300
[12] S. S. Newman, "Further Experiments in Phonetic Symbolism", in

Journal of Experimental Psychology, XII, p 225

¹³ *General Anthropology*, NY, 1938, p 132

¹⁴ quoted in O. Rank, *Art and Artist*, 1932, p 237

¹⁵ Benjamin Lee Whorf, "Relation of Thought and Behavior to Language", in *Four Articles in Metalinguistics*, p 83

¹⁶ *PhdSF*, Vol I, p 110

¹⁷ *ibid.*, Vol II, p 122

¹⁸ *Das Templum*, Leipzig, 1869

¹⁹ *PhdSF*, Vol II, p 129

²⁰ quoted in Phd SF, 11, pp 118, 130, 181, 184, 230

²¹ Ernst Mach, *Erkenntnis und Irrtum*, p 334

²² *Principles of Psychology*, Vol II, p 237

²³ *ibid.*, p 238

²⁴ *ibid.*, p 246

²⁵ *Mathematische Annalen*, Vol. 43

²⁶ quoted in: H. Hartmann, *Gestalt-Psychology*, p 106

²⁷ *ibid.*

²⁸ B. Russell, *Mysticism and Logic*, p 92

²⁹ Ernest Nagel, "Impossible Numbers", in *Studies in the History of Ideas*, Vol V, p 470

³⁰ *Nouveaux Essais*; Book IV, ch. 4

³¹ *PhdSF*, Vol. III, p 490

³² Ernest Nagel, "Impossible Numbers", in studies in the History of Ideas Vol V, p 471

CHAPTER VI

¹ *Collected Paers*, ed. Hartshorne and Weiss, Vol. II, p 330

² "Foundations of the Theory of Signs", in *Internatl. Encycl. of Unified Science*, 1938, Vol I, p 2

³ *ibid.*, p 4

⁴ *PhdSF*, Vol I, p 18

⁵ *ibid.*

⁶ E. Husserl, *Logische Untersuchungen*, Vol II, p 23

⁷ John Dewey, *Logic; Theory of Inquiry*, p 51–52

⁸ *Philosophy in a New Key*, pp 58, 61

⁹ Charles Morris, *Signs, Language and Behavior*, p 50–52

¹⁰ *Language and Myth*, Langer transl., pp 8, 11

¹¹ Charles Morris, *Foundations of a Theory of Signs*, p 24

¹² "Foundations of Logic and Mathematics", in *Internatl. Encycl. of Unified Science*, Chicago, 1939, p 6

¹³ Charles Morris, *Foundations etc.*, p 4

¹⁴ *ibid.*, pp 43–48

¹⁵ *Language and Myth*, p 24

¹⁶ *Language and Myth*, Langer transl., pp 24, 25

¹⁷ "Personal Values as Selective Factors in Perception", in *Journal of Abnormal and Social Psychology*, 1948, p 142

¹⁸ Hans Reichenbach, in *Logos*, 1920

¹⁹ Philip Frank, in *Theoria*, 1938, Vol VI

²⁰ *Four Articles in Metalinguistics*, Washington DC (undated) p 91

²¹ *Language and Myth*, Langer transl.; p 38

²² "Götternamen", quoted from Langer transl. of *Language and Myth*, p 16

²³ "Die Sprache und der Aufbau der Gegenstandswelt"; *Bericht über den XII. Kongress der Deutschen Gesellschaft fuer Psychologie.*, Fischer, Hamburg-Jena, 1932

²⁴ C. W. Mills, "Language, Logic and Culture", in *American Sociological Review*, 1939, p 677

[25] *Human Nature*, p 216
[26] *Four Articles in Metalinguistics*, Washington, DC, (undated), p 11
[27] *ibid.* p 5
[28] Karl Buehler, *Die geistige Entwicklung des Kindes*, Jena, 1921, p 128
[29] *PhdSF*, Vol. III, p 141
[30] Hans Reichenbach, *Experience and Prediction*, Chicago, 1938, p 195
[31] *An Essay on Man*, p 35
[32] K. Carnap, *Foundations of Logic and Mathematics*, p 6
[33] *ibid.*
[34] Hans Reichenbach, *Experience and Prediction*, p 4
[35] Lindsay and Margenau, *The Foundation of Physics*, NY, 1936, p 12
[36] Hans Reichenbach, *Experience and Prediction*, p 7
[37] in his *Logic*, part I
[38] Felix Kaufman, *Methodology of the Social Sciences*, Oxford, 1944, pp 67, 72
[39] *Tractatus Logico-Philosophicus*, The Humanities Press, Inc., London, 1951, p 188 (Prop. 7)
[40] *Theoria*, 1938, p 158
[41] A. Pap, *The Apriori in Physical Theory*, NY, 1946
[42] *Zur Logik der Kulturwissenschaften*, 1942; p 30
[43] *ibid.*
[44] *Theoria*, 1938, p 173
[45] "The Influence of Language upon the Development of Scientific Thought", in *Journal of Philosophy*, NY, XXXIX, p 12
[46] S. K. Langer, *Philosophy in a New Key*, pp 21, 22

CHAPTER VII

[1] Berkeley and Los Angeles, 1951, p 276
[2] D. T. Suzuki, "Reason and Intuition in Buddhist Philosophy", in *Essays in East-West Philosophy*, Univ. of Hawai, 1951, p 36
[3] *Principles etc.*, par. 65
[4] *Principles of Psychology*, Vol II, p 237
[5] see also E. G. Mesthene's "On the status of the laws of logic." In: *Philosophy and Phaenomenological Research;* Vol. X, No 3; pp 354-372. (1950)
[6] for a fuller discussion, see the author's "Psychology and the Ethics of Survival". In: *Philosophy of Science;* Vol. 23, No. 23; pp 82-89 (1956)

INDEX

NAMES

SUBJECTS

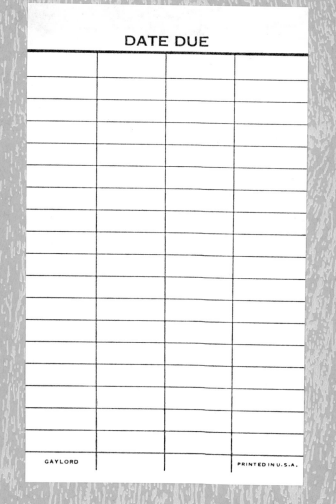

DATE DUE

GAYLORD			PRINTED IN U.S.A.